Timothy Gillum & Kery Mortenson

# PERFORMANCE EATING RABBITS

*What B.O.L.D. People See and Do*

outskirts press

Outskirts Press, Inc.
http://www.outskirtspress.com

ISBN: 978-1-4787-9392-2

Illustrations by Kayla D. Potter. All rights reserved - used with permission.

Outskirts Press and the "OP" logo are trademarks belonging to Outskirts Press, Inc.

PRINTED IN THE UNITED STATES OF AMERICA

# TABLE OF CONTENTS

Foreword ..................................................................................i

Preface...................................................................................v

Introduction: What BOLD People See and Do ..............................ix

Chapter 1: Performance-Eating Rabbits (PERs) ........................... 1

Chapter 2: Organizational Truths................................................ 17

Chapter 3: Pain-Free Vision Statement ....................................... 24

Chapter 4: Trapping the One-Hit-Wonder Wabbit........................ 32

Chapter 5: Speed Dating for Solutions ....................................... 45

Chapter 6: The Strategic F Word................................................. 52

Chapter 7: Building Behavior Bridges .......................................... 69

Chapter 8: Ledge Walking........................................................... 76

Chapter 9: Paying it forward....................................................... 91

Chapter 10: Tools Workbook ...................................................... 98

References:............................................................................... 129

# FOREWORD

I've had the opportunity to hear Tim and Kery tell their story of how they use performance improvement principles to change the institutionalized (yet no longer effective) behaviors of work teams. With each presentation, they invariably hold up a stuffed brown rabbit as a metaphor that this work is not something you pull out of your a\*\*. Instead, it is a process of uncovering what is really going on; helping people reflect and then confront the futility of doing the same thing, while expecting different results. They tell stories based on real examples of how they, through their jovial but frank style, get groups to come to grips with the fact that what they really do (yet what they tell themselves they do) are not the same. Tim and Kery have developed methods and tools that quickly uncover the truth. They use story and metaphor to help groups create new possibilities and new ways of working to get better results. This book presents the tools they use. It is peppered with stories, quotes, and wisdom we can all use to create new ways of helping work groups be more effective.

It is not often that I get the opportunity to read a book that is informative, provocative, useful, and funny. Kery and Tim have done an exceptional job of balancing purposeful content with inviting questions of reflection coupled with practical handouts. Add *Performance-Eating Rabbits* to your must-read list.

Judith Hale, PhD, CPT, CACP, CIDD

### Do you need this book?

Follow three easy steps to decide:

Answer the following questions below by circling Yes or No.

| Question | Answer |
|---|---|
| 1. Are you leading or supporting improvement initiatives that are at risk for failure? | Yes  No |
| 2. Are you interested in solutions that are easier and more effective? | Yes  No |
| 3. Do you face challenges trying to transform your team, leaders or culture? | Yes  No |
| 4. Are you looking for a better way to enhance team effectiveness? | Yes  No |
| 5. Would you like to take the guesswork out of seeing real behavior change? | Yes  No |
| 6. Do you find it challenging to create your mission/vision? | Yes  No |
| 7. Would you like transform your team from "Order Taker" to "Difference Maker?" | Yes  No |
| 8. Do you need a faster process to develop solutions that really work? | Yes  No |
| 9. Would you like to develop a robust strategy in four hours? | Yes  No |

Step 1: If you answered "yes" to any of these questions, this book is for you!

Step 2: If you answered "yes" to four or more questions, you should purchase several copies of this book (for you and your fellow colleagues).

Step 3: If you answered "yes" to six or more questions, read the book and then contact us as soon as possible.

# Preface

*"The meaning of life is to find your gift.*
*The purpose of life is to give it away."*

*~ Pablo Picasso*

**The current landscape** of our professional and personal lives is full of new and exciting challenges to navigate. Whether we are professionals in the fields of learning, organizational development, performance improvement or simply someone giving selflessly to one of the many great causes in our world, we are driven to align our skills, passions and values to the mission of the organization. We are also in the middle of significant challenges: a generational changing-of-the-guard with respect to workforce and societal leadership; the evolution of technology at a more rapid rate than ever before; and increased scrutiny resulting from questionable practices within several industries.

Thus, we are tasked with ensuring each of us (and our teams) are ready to meet the challenges of today, while keeping pace with change and remaining competitive in the global economy. The increasing relevance and interest in this topic centers on the need to evolve the tools and processes of our craft. This is imperative to meet the increasing business and societal demands of speed, innovation and agility.

This publication provides a colorful road map to rapidly drive transformational results. We leverage a creative and measurable blend of performance technology tools that align with the strategic needs and underlying purpose of the organization. The innovative nature of this conceptual blend breathes new life into the tried and true standard tools of learning, organizational development and performance technology. It also leverages measurement tools and impactful story-telling techniques. The practical application of this process rapidly enables the reader to identify, select, communicate, implement and measure a strategic plan (while keeping a pulse on the cultural fabric of the organization). Each of these systematic stages of the performance technology process presents readers with challenges we like to call "ledges." It is these ledges that we must rapidly decide to either pull our organization *from*, or simply push them *off,* while always being aware of the dangers the "Performance-Eating Rabbits" present.

*Our purpose is three-fold:*

We first introduce the critical steps necessary for navigating the performance pitfalls we encounter every day. Tangible examples are used to articulate the importance of what we can do to help avert situations where a pre-determined solution is implemented prematurely, often leading to undesirable results.

Secondly, practical reflection questions are included, enabling the reader to move to performer (or action-taker). We encourage thinking deeply and truthfully regarding each reflection question, and we provide a section to record answers for future use.

The final purpose of this book is to provide simple and powerful tools with step-by-step instructions to help the reader do the work and achieve success for themselves, their clients, their organizations and, most importantly, the performers that are trying to navigate the many ledges they encounter.

## How to Use this Book

This book can be read in different ways based on your need, experience level and your genuine curiosity. Some of you will read this book cover to cover and actively engage in every reflection and activity. Some of you will skip straight to the last chapter to use the tools and templates we provide. Others of you will read, practice and apply specific chapters that immediately address your most pressing needs or match your curiosity level. No matter what your approach may be, we fully expect you will apply the concepts, tools and processes covered here, achieving impactful results. Please don't limit your exploration of this material to your work environment. The concepts and tools presented are also transferable to individuals working on improving human performance within academic, social and family settings.

Each chapter will include an explanation of the chapter concepts, followed by a self-reflection activity to help ground you in your current state with the concepts. We will then share some of our stories, applying the concepts to real life challenges we face. We see these challenges as the wild, crazy and elusive "rabbits" that we have visualized, named and established effective ways of mitigating. We then turn our focus to introduce and provide opportunities to practice the tool(s) and principle(s) of each chapter, and apply them to your current situation. We end each chapter with an opportunity for you to build an action plan to leverage what you have just experienced. For ongoing use of this book, all our tools (with instructions) are included in the final chapter.

Simply reading this book will not replace the transformational learning you will experience through the successes, failures, and barriers encountered each time you apply these concepts. Try not to be content with an initial success or dejected by a set-back. Life is a long journey, filled with ample opportunities to apply these concepts to all aspects of our lives. With this in mind, we wish you happy reading.

## ACKNOWLEDGEMENTS

We first want to thank you for purchasing this book and benefiting from what we have put together. We hope to meet you someday and hear about your experiences. You can reach us at www.performancejourneypartners.net if you would like to share your feedback (good or bad). We see feedback as a gift.

We want to thank the individuals who prompted, challenged and taunted us into getting lift-off with this book. We greatly appreciate the talented professionals who graciously agreed to read our manuscript, share their insight, wisdom and experience. We hope to be more like them when we grow up.

JUST a special and HUGE thank you to Rebecca Potter-Hill for her time, talents and propensity to dot every I and cross every T. She is absolutely one of the BOLDest individuals we know!

Last, but not least, we appreciate our spouses and family members who kept us in the pocket and supported us in every way possible!

*Tim & Kery*

# Introduction:
# What **BOLD** People See and Do

*"All of your dreams can come
true if you pursue them."*

**~ Walt Disney**

**As performance improvement** leaders, we have both the gift and
the curse of being able to see an entire system. As a result, we
have the challenge of being tempted by the god of "big wins."
We must be BOLD in our approach to harnessing our gifts,
while keeping our expectations in check, as we drive our organizations closer to the ultimate prize. This chapter will describe
how the book is organized, briefly explain the main points of
each chapter, and solidify the need to be BOLD in our approach.
Additionally, it will creatively reinforce the enormous power of
the quick and simple.

## Tim's Insight

One of my favorite stories growing up was Stone Soup. My
mother often read this book to me at bedtime in the hopes that I
would drift off to sleep and afford her the much-needed break she
so deserved and longed for. The general premise of the book is that
a traveler noticed the entire village was hungry, and one wealthy individual held all the food in his cellar. The traveler understood that

the greedy individual had all of the resources required to make a soup that would more than satisfy the hunger of the entire village. The wealthy individual was letting his greed and self-centered view on life drive his behavior. The traveler helped this individual break from his selfish ways by convincing him he could make the best-tasting soup (that would feed the entire village) with just a cauldron of water and one stone.

He stirred the water and stone, tasting it and bragging to the greedy man of how good it tasted. The man wanted a taste, but the traveler informed him that it was a great soup and it would be even better if he had a ham bone. Out of curiosity, the greedy man went to his cellar to grab a ham bone to add to the soup. The traveler tasted the soup and bragged how good it tasted, but how much better it would be with some potatoes. The miser retrieved the potatoes, and this back-and-forth continued for another twenty ingredients. (Sometimes it was fifteen, depending on how tired my mom was.) In the end, through curiosity, patience, creativity and a deep understanding of the desired end result, the traveler accepted a series of small wins to feed the entire village. He harnessed the power of the quick and simple.

Unfortunately for my mom, the story generally engaged my imagination in such a way that I peppered her with a litany of questions and *"what ifs"* that applied to the things I was experiencing. How could I use this approach in school, in sports, at church (or to con my brother into sharing that candy he had hoarded in his room)? This curiosity has carried over into my adult life. I find myself seeking to understand what my current "village" needs and how I can break this potentially large and complex need into simple ingredients that will enable me to meet it. Sometimes we work with individuals who have all the knowledge, tools, resources, vision or authority stored in their cellar -- and we need to find ways to gain access to these organizational ingredients to drive our organizations forward, one ingredient at a time if we must.

*Reader Reflection*
_____

- *In your organization, what is the real need of the "village?"*
- *What are the key ingredients (processes, resources, authority, etc.) you must acquire to meet this need?*
- *Who are the owners of these ingredients?*
- *How can you pique the curiosity of these individuals to contribute to your "organizational Soup?"*

*BOLD-ly go where no man (or woman) has gone before*

In addition to seeing the system and its components, we also must be BOLD in our approach to establish, drive and measure the strategy of our organizations. What is BOLD? It is a simple acronym that provides a framework for describing the behaviors exemplar strategists exhibit, while driving results that can (and should be) achieved in their organization. BOLD is simply:

**B –** Be authentic to your core values – regardless of your circumstances.
**O –** Open-minded to new ideas and ways of thinking.
**L –** Lead with courage and humility.
**D –** Define new standards for excellence and performance in yourself and others.

Being authentic in your core values requires you to fully understand who you are and be comfortable enough to let the organization see the real you. In today's world of political correctness and fear of offending, this is no small task. We sometimes take on different personas for home, work, school and other social settings to be accepted. We even take on multiple personas within different project teams or meetings. To deliver a robust strategy, you need to be comfortable in your own skin and be willing to be loved, hated or challenged in the moment.

### Being Authentic to your Core Values: Kery's Insight

I have a friend named Jeff, a very successful account executive. He could sell Alaska orange futures to farmers in Florida! He is intelligent, knows his products inside and out, and is well versed in the larger market dynamics. Jeff has something that makes him even more prominent; he demonstrated BOLD long before we had given it a name. He would openly share his expertise with others – even to those who were his competitors. If there was an issue that could tarnish his company, he would lead with courage to get the solution resolved, always exceeding customer expectations. Behind the scenes, he also volunteered with several large non-profit organizations. He defined standards of excellence in himself before comparing his performance against others.

A core value that made Jeff stand out to me was his ability to do the right thing, the right way, for the right purpose. In simple terms, Jeff was being authentic (the first BOLD attribute) regardless of his circumstances, and often without being noticed.

On one occasion when I saw this in action, Jeff was meeting with his key clients, who were interested in purchasing one of his major products. Jeff described the benefits of his instrument confidently, but without being arrogant. I could tell they trusted him and were ready to make the purchase. He could have easily taken the order and his commission, but he didn't close the deal. When I asked him why, his response was profound. He said he knew they really wanted his product, but he saw a negative impact on the overall profit to their operation (which his customers did not even see). Jeff proposed a better solution for them would be sharing the expense with a similar organization. Ultimately, it would lower their operation cost while providing the same level of service. Jeff understood the larger picture.

How about you, will you be authentic to your core, or will you simply be an "order taker?" You may be successful in rallying teams and achieving a high degree of excellence in your field of work or service. But, we are challenging you to kick it up a notch beyond the gold standard, to the BOLD standard of performance.

*Open-Minded to New Ideas*

Tim has found that there are only two people in this world who know everything. Who you might ask? They are his wife and his mother, and you are neither. Success is dependent on your ability to understand that many roads will take you to the same destination, and exploring several of them will enable you to find the fastest, most effective and actionable path. An open mind is extremely helpful in earning buy-in and support from your key stakeholders. To paraphrase the great Albert Einstein, *"We cannot expect to do things the way they have always been done and expect different results."*

*Lead with Courage and Humility*

**Leading the pack with courage and humility ensures that you do not fall victim to your fears or to your ego.** Leading with actions, words and presence is what aligns our strategic actions with the urgency of our organizations. We will not fear the new, unknown challenges, and we will not let our egos hinder our progress just for security or self-gain. Your success in leading the pack will be judged by each and every person you encounter throughout your life. Don't be afraid of this scrutiny. Embrace it and lead with courage and humility.

*Define New Standards for Excellence*

Defining new standards of excellence will enable you to continuously improve yourself and your organization. While you will celebrate success and learn from challenges and failures, you must continue to raise the bar. Look for best practices from other organizations and leaders, and then build upon them. First raise the bar of *your* standards, and then leverage the power of "stone soup" to drive your curiosity in redefining what excellence really looks like.

**Defining new standards of excellence will enable you to continuously improve yourself and your organization.**

An example of ordinary people defining new standards of excellence was shared with us when we facilitated a teambuilding event for sales professionals. Our purpose was to create an awareness with the audience of what it takes to deliver high quality service to customers. At the event, we had participants get into groups, asking each person to share an experience in which they delivered and/or were the recipient of an over-the-top customer experience. Each group identified one exceptional example from their discussion that made the experience unforgettable. We were not ready for the intensity and depth of the stories shared. Here is one that stood out.

A medical sales representative was making a routine call at an oncology hospital. The head oncologist told him about a patient (a young child who was terminally ill). The family wanted to fly to their home in South America with their child, to be with the rest of their family during this difficult time. They had been informed the medical device necessary for keeping the child alive during the flight home would not perform properly at high altitudes, so a flight would not be possible. Once the salesman realized there was an issue, he quickly researched his competitor's products and found a device that would work, and put them immediately in touch with the oncologist.

When the sales professional returned several weeks later for a follow-up, the entire oncology team was waiting for him with a thank-you banner and were applauding wildly, recognizing him for going the extra mile that helped the child safely make the trip.

The sales representative made a lasting impact on his customers, (and more importantly, the patient and family). He set a new standard of excellence, which his fellow colleagues applauded. Upon hearing this story, many people at the team building event were teary-eyed and motivated to live up to the new standard.

Demonstrating BOLD behaviors in your organization will provide significant outcomes that catalyze sustainable value for your customers. It can unleash an innovative and rewarding experience for your entire workforce. It is not difficult to grasp the concept of being BOLD. However, being BOLD requires you to be constantly self-aware, able to treat feedback (good or bad) as a gift, and maintain your spirit of curiosity. Recognizing where you are in each moment will help maintain your self-awareness and enable you to navigate many of the challenges associated with improving performance.

> **Demonstrating BOLD behaviors in your organization will provide significant outcomes that catalyze sustainable value for your customers.**

## Reader Reflection

If you looked at yourself in a mirror when you are being BOLD (and also when you are not), what would you see?

- *What are you doing?*
- *What are you saying?*
- *What are others saying about you?*
- *What results are you achieving?*
- *How does it feel?*

Record your responses in the following table.

| | What you look like when you are BOLD | What you look like when you are **not** BOLD |
|---|---|---|
| **Be** Authentic to Your Core Values | | |
| **O**pen-Minded to New Ideas | | |
| **L**ead with Courage and Humility | | |
| **D**efine New Standards of Excellence | | |

## *Overview*

The concepts, tools and processes in this book are designed to help us navigate the performance challenges facing teams and organizations, while ensuring they strategically thrive in the future. In the first chapter of this book, we introduce you to some pesky little things that keep us from taking action or from finishing what we start. They may even begin eating at the fabric of who we are. We call these pesky friends *Performance-Eating Rabbits*. The second chapter explains how to gain a deeper understanding of the ground truth of our teams and organizations, while quickly building trust that ignites success. The third chapter teaches you how to take the pain out of vision statements, and chapter four focuses on how to identify the barriers that keep teams from achieving their desired state. Chapter five leverages the fun and excitement of speed dating to quickly identify powerful solutions. The book then shifts focus in chapter six, breathing new life into the tried, true, and often misaligned SWOT analysis. Chapters seven and eight provide the opportunity to learn new ways of approaching culture, and the many ledges of success and failure. Chapter nine gives insight on how to pay it forward for yourself, your team, and organization. It concludes with a call to action. The final chapter includes an easy to use reference guide (Tools Workbook) which provides the instructions we describe throughout the book.

## Chapter Recap

Harnessing the power of the "quick and simple," and also being BOLD are foundational to apply the concepts, tools and processes provided in this book. The first quick and simple action you can take occurs when you look into the mirror in the morning. You need to see the BOLD person you truly are and commit to seeking the real needs of your village. Whether it is at work, at home or in your community, boldly search for the recipe that will successfully feed your village. As you search out the key ingredients to your strategic success, be aware of those *Performance-Eating Rabbits.* The next chapter of this book will help you identify, manage and mitigate those pesky varmints.

# CHAPTER 1
# PERFORMANCE-EATING RABBITS (PERS)

*"The people who are crazy enough to think they can change the world are the ones who do."*

**~ Albert Einstein**

Creating robust improvement can be daunting and difficult. At times, you may feel like the magician who must quickly and magically pull a rabbit out of a hat!

While we wish we could make results happen like a magician, more often the *Performance-Eating Rabbits* (PERs) are not cute or cuddly. They often are *not* pulled from a hat. They emerge from a different orifice - hence a brown *Performance-Eating Rabbit* has emerged along with their performance-eating cousins. Yikes!! Rabbits of this variety have one priority: to devour and destroy the performance you were hoping to achieve and/or sustain in your organization.

> The *Performance-Eating Rabbits* (PERs) are not cute or cuddly. They often are *not* pulled from a hat. They emerge from a different orifice

*Performance-Eating Rabbits* **come in many different types, sizes and appetites**. They are hungry and anxious to eat your improvement initiatives early and often. PERs live in your sphere of influence and may be difficult to spot. They blend in easily with their surroundings. These furry creatures could already be wreaking havoc and preventing new innovative ideas. They swiftly derail

1

the outcomes you were hoping to achieve. If you are complacent with the status quo and allow PERs to exist, they will derail any chance of achieving success for your enterprise.

Through our experiences, we have identified and characterized seven types of *Performance-Eating Rabbits*. This chapter provides insight on how to recognize each PER, their characteristics, and how they work both independently and in concert with other PERs.

In your experiences, you may have encountered other types of PERs. We believe the tools in this book will help you mitigate those as well. It is critical that you quickly catch and render them incapable of destroying your strategy. Note: You may choose to catch and release them to your competitors and let them chomp on their hopes for success.

We will provide a dossier of each PER that includes:

- How they operate to undermine success
- When they multiply
- Key actions to minimize their impact

*The Famous Seven Performance-Eating Rabbits (PERs)*

- Political Rabbit
- Hasty Hopper
- One-Hit-Wonder Wabbit
- Bias Bunny
- Complacent Bunny
- Culture Rabbit
- Ledge-Walking Rabbit

**Political Rabbits** tend to be out front of the other PERs. These rabbits promote their current flavor of the month, tagging on their ideas to buzz-words that sound good, however, will not motivate or unleash the workforce. The result is less quality, productivity, and efficiency. In the end, it results in valuable contributors losing hope, taking their ball and going home, or leaving to play for the competition.

If your *Political Rabbits* are perceived as a threat (instead of an opportunity), they can turn a pro-active culture into a reactive and defensive workforce -- focused on avoiding action, blaming others, and more importantly, not doing the real work that is critical for success.

*Political Rabbits* demonstrate excellent communication skills. They use smooth sounding words, like employee engagement, agility, big data, strong leadership, inclusive workforce, and other endless clichés. They refer to the people in the organization as "headcount" (aka "head lettuce") or something that can be moved, re-purposed, minimized, or eliminated altogether. They've mastered the ability to say one thing to their audience, then can contradict what they say to another group within the same organization. They believe their voice is more important than the voices of others. They are so persistent and influential, they could get mentioned in Dilbert cartoons and yet come out unscathed!

> **If your *Political Rabbits* are perceived as a threat (instead of an opportunity), they can turn a pro-active culture into a reactive and defensive workforce**

The *Political Rabbit* exerts the ability to influence outcomes. They focus power to affect decisions that are self-serving, or attempt to influence outcomes to provide advantage for themselves. They also influence situations to pose a disadvantage for others. The daily dose of disseminating rumors and half-truths occurs quickly and sometimes without notice. They will withhold information until the right opportunity presents itself to achieve their advantage. They may befriend *Culture Rabbits* if the trust level is low. The bonding between Political and Culture Rabbits is always stronger in organizations with low trust.

The breeding season for *Political Rabbits* typically occurs during end-of-year performance reviews, or when there are subjective criteria in talent appraisals, minimal constructive feedback, and vague expectations about job roles. *Political Rabbits* increase their activity when there is demonstrated low employee satisfaction, downsizing, or change of resources leading to role ambiguity.

PERs of this variety lack self-awareness. They serve as key stakeholders without a stake. (They used the last stake to stab others who got in their way.) They have no problem eating their young, as long as it achieves their ultimate goal!

*Actions to minimize the Political Rabbits*

---

- ✓ *Foster a strong trust level within the workforce and leadership.*
- ✓ *Encourage everyone, regardless of title and role, to constructively and respectfully challenge opinions and ideas.*
- ✓ *Recognize and reward ideas that make doing the right thing easy and the wrong thing difficult.*
- ✓ *Eliminate unhealthy competition, especially in critical roles.*

**Hasty Hoppers** are hopping fast so you barely see them. They are focused on doing the expedient thing over the right thing. They are obsessed with achieving speed and efficiency in whatever they do.

They can be helpful to your strategy on the front end (to generate faster results). If you are using the tools correctly that we recommend in this book, they should stay out of your way and allow your strategy to progress forward. They will get testy if it is taking you months to make decisions and develop your plan to move forward.

They are poor listeners, and interrupt workers frequently to let them know how slow they are going about their tasks. They recognize workers who achieve short wins, but often reward them with more work. This cycle continues until the incentive runs out of gas due to exhaustion, leaving a trail of low retention, fear **_Hasty Hoppers_ have multiplication down to a science.** and distrust. Oh yes, we must not forget to mention, over-worked employees!

*Hasty Hoppers* have multiplication down to a science. When needed, they are fast and furious. They increase when the organization creates a sense of urgency. As mentioned earlier, they can be an ally if your strategy involves efficient process improvement. However, too much of a good thing may cause this *Hasty Hopper* to be more performance eating than performance supporting.

*Hasty Hoppers* multiply at the front end of your strategy. Sometimes they co-produce with the *One-Hit-Wonder Wabbit* to speed things up -- stay tuned!

*Actions to minimize Hasty Hoppers*

---

- ✓ *Keep your strategy simple with performance outcomes that involve both efficiency and effectiveness.*
- ✓ *Leverage their expertise for developing the key predictive indicators for success.*
- ✓ *Apply robust and efficient gap analysis and solution selection process prior to execution.*

**One-Hit-Wonder Wabbit** – This PER supports only one solution for any initiative.

*One-Hit Wonder Rabbits* argue that their solution is needed to improve the current problem. They fail to see a bigger system that is impacting an already skilled workforce, which may be bogged down by other factors. For example, they send messages to the managers convincing

them the key to company success is re-training the workforce.

They firmly believe in a single solution. And the one they select tends to be their favorite. They impact strategy by eating valuable time and money. We frequently see the *One-Hit-Wonder Wabbits* leave the enterprise before their solution is completed (for obvious reasons). They don't want to be blamed for a failed solution. They blame the *Culture Rabbit* for the implementation failure or blame the *Complacent Bunny* for not joining their cause. The *Political Rabbit* will simply say, "*I told you so,*" and now you are left with a one-legged strategy that gridlocks your enterprise.

**They fail to describe the real issue or additional solutions that may aid in solving the problem.**

We like to debate with the *One-Hit-Wonder Wabbit*. However, they can come at you fast and passionate with their out-of-the-blue solution. They fail to describe the real issue or additional solutions that may aid in solving the problem.

Their season for multiplying typically increases at the front end of the initiative, or whenever solutions are discussed. They flourish when an enterprise adopts a common goal with no roadmap or description for completion.

*The One-Hit-Wonder Wabbit at work:*

A corporate leader declared the solution to performance im-provement was for every employee to complete a minimum of forty hours training per year. This is simple to measure if you are only tracking the hours completed. The real question that should have been asked is "*Will forty hours of training actually produce the desired outcomes the leader was hoping for?*" If asked, our re-sponse would have been "*Since when did people in our company become stupid and thus require forty hours of un-targeted learn-ing events? Have we thought about the tax (time & money) to the organization?*"

The *One-Hit-Wonder Wabbit* had already hopped over to the leader and planted his solution in the leader's long term memory. Before you know it – the solution was sanctioned. Those in the training organization were on the butt end (literally) to deliver the solution that would tax the enterprise and then label them as the fall guys when the actual results came in.

*Actions to minimize the One-Hit-Wonder Wabbit*

---

- ✓ *Encourage your team to avoid jumping to solutions without first analyzing the causal factors for the current state.*
- ✓ *Implement a structured approach for cause analysis regarding the current state prior to defining the solutions for your initiative.*
- ✓ *Prevent the One-Hit-Wonder Wabbit from dominating conversations with open discussion of the ground truth.*
- ✓ *Listen and encourage the voices in the room who have not yet spoken.*

The **Bias Bunny** seems tame on the outside, however, they have a passive/aggressive demeanor when it comes to identifying innovative solutions to address problems. *Bias Bunnies* have a preconceived notion of the issue and tend to discredit the fact there is even a problem. If they have enough authority, they easily discredit the ideas of others. They promote ideas they believe in. They will take full credit for the initial success and then pass on the blame when the results fizzle. They have a pessimistic attitude, which may have been introduced to them by their Culture or Political relatives. There is strong evidence the *Bias Bunny* and *Culture Rabbit* are close cousins.

They exhibit great effort to discredit the innovative ideas of others. Their math skills are creative, as metrics seem to change to fit their story. They may pull information, often out of context, to support their view. Although *Bias Bunnies* do not multiply as frequently as the *Culture Rabbits*, they flourish when an enterprise adopts a common goal with no clear roadmap linked to results.

*Actions to minimize the Bias Bunny*

---

- ✓ *Include everyone in identifying solutions for your strategy.*
- ✓ *Solicit team solutions through an efficient process that is non-threatening.*
- ✓ *Identify the effort and benefit of each solution before deciding on actions.*
- ✓ *Identify early leading indicators or results of the proposed solutions.*

 **Complacent Bunnies** are so tiny, at first you may not know they even exist. They say little, unless they are hungry and need more carrots. If they are fed in their organization, they are content with whatever happens and they will not be a serious threat. They are self-centered. They will participate in teams, but will not significantly contribute. They will back away from making waves with other PERs.

Initially, they will shy away from challenging conversations. They commit to change if it doesn't cause them fear of losing something they already value. If that happens, they will not engage in supporting the new direction. If their safety net is challenged, they take sides with the *Political Rabbit,* who promises them safety. If threatened, they can go into hiding with a passive/aggressive mentality, causing division.

8

Their breeding season tends to be somewhat rare. (After all – they are complacent bunnies.) If there is turnover or downsizing, you may see more of them show up. They increase if they find a group of sympathizing *Bias Bunnies* or *Ledge-Walking Rabbits* to hang out with.

*Actions to minimize the Complacent Bunnies*

---

- ✓ *Encourage open and honest conversation – with guidelines for keeping it safe.*
- ✓ *Encourage the complacent participants to openly speak.*
- ✓ *Explain that the risk of staying at "status quo" has significant consequences.*
- ✓ *Include the favorable outcomes they can receive by being fully engaged.*

The **Culture Rabbit** is king and the largest of the PER 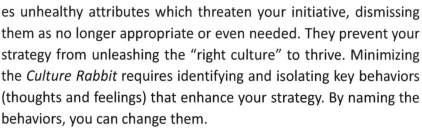 family. *Culture Rabbits* are not necessarily seen or heard (like the Political Rabbits), but have an overwhelming and ominous influence, preventing positive change by keeping everything "status quo." Peter Drucker identified the huge impact of the *Culture Rabbit* when he coined the phrase "culture eats strategy for breakfast." If your environment is undergoing rapid change, the *Culture Rabbit* establishes unhealthy attributes which threaten your initiative, dismissing them as no longer appropriate or even needed. They prevent your strategy from unleashing the "right culture" to thrive. Minimizing the *Culture Rabbit* requires identifying and isolating key behaviors (thoughts and feelings) that enhance your strategy. By naming the behaviors, you can change them.

Their multiplication is a daily and ongoing occurrence. They can be more noticeable and vocal when initiatives with a chance of success are receiving early adoption. They stop reproducing when complacency sets in. If there is leadership turnover, *Culture Rabbits* may go into hiding. This happens not because of fear, but strategically, to make it more difficult for new leadership to implement change. They are skilled at destroying improvement strategies and they are ferocious eaters. If your strategy has the right sauce, it can be seen as a tasty morsel!

**Minimizing the *Culture Rabbit* requires identifying and isolating key behaviors (thoughts and feelings) that enhance your strategy.**

We believe people are smart, after all, they are your company's greatest asset (or possibly your worst nightmare). They are quick to pick up on cues that give them a picture of the culture makeup. We tend to think only long-time employees are affected by the *Culture Rabbits* influence. Think again! *Culture Rabbits* thrive from day one of new employee on-boarding sessions, since individuals leading the session have already been inoculated with the culture serum or already drank the cultural juice. They articulate vivid stories that engrain *"This is how it's really done here!"* *Culture Rabbits* leverage their prowess with *Political Rabbits* and *Complacent Bunnies*, having intelligence that rivals the Central Intelligence Agency.

*Actions to minimize Culture Rabbits*

- ✓ *Foster a strong positive culture that aligns with the organization's values.*
- ✓ *Encourage everyone to challenge solutions that may conflict with their values.*
- ✓ *Recognize front-line leaders and workers who demonstrate your counter- culture attributes. This assumes your leadership already demonstrates this!*
- ✓ *Eliminate unhealthy competition that would impede trust.*

✓ Share stories about the benefits of a new and different desired state.
✓ Clarify the connections between the organization's strategy and those of the individual employee.
✓ Encourage employees to identify their purpose in shaping a different culture.

The **Ledge-Walking Rabbit** has a desire to see your organization flourish, but may not have the tools or knowhow to make the right changes necessary for success. The *Ledge-Walking Rabbit* eagerly comes on board, bringing new ideas to make an impact. They are initially successful; however, they can easily get ensnared in the agendas of other PERs. (After all, they are in the same family.) The *Ledge-Walking Rabbit* can become a formidable ally for your improvement initiatives. But, they can also potentially make poor decisions; causing additional problems for your enterprise and workers, which in the end yields minimal improvement.

*Ledge-Walking Rabbits* can easily succumb to what's called "*Squirrel Syndrome*," which we have defined as: *The act of losing focus on the strategic task at hand, when a new and seemingly "real cool" idea runs right in front of us. This is the human version of how dogs stop everything and anything they are doing to chase a squirrel.*

If there is an initiative in your organization that is shinier or more visible, they will immediately *hop-on* to other initiatives that require their time and attention.

The breeding season of *Ledge-Walking Rabbits* typically occurs at the beginning of your initiative. This can be positive since they immediately want to contribute. But when difficult situations or conversations arise, they may go into hiding or follow the Squirrel Syndrome.

> *Ledge-Walking Rabbits* **can easily succumb to** **what's called** *"Squirrel Syndrome"*

*Actions to minimize Ledge-Walking Rabbits*

---

- ✓ *Explain the risk of status quo.*
- ✓ *Use a blend of qualitative and quantitative data.*
- ✓ *Validate your strategy with internal and external factors.*
- ✓ *Share your strategy in detail before you start down the path.*
- ✓ *Be ready to engage them in conversation if they start hopping toward a squirrel.*

*Reader Reflection on the Seven Famous Performance-Eating Rabbits*

---

- *Have you encountered a PER in your work?*
- *What type of PER was it?*
- *What actions did you take to mitigate their effect and was it successful?*

*Reader Practice*

---

Instructions: Rate your level of expertise for questions 1and 2, then record your comments and insight for questions 3, 4 and 5.

1. How **effective** are your strategies to move your organization in a new and better direction? *(circle your response)*
   Lousy        Poor        Average        Pretty good        Great

2. How **efficient** are your strategies to move your organization in a new and better direction? *(circle your response)*
   Lousy        Poor        Average        Pretty good        Great

3. What PERs are impacting your success?

4. What are you doing about it?

5.  Have you knowingly or unknowingly participated with PERs? Which one(s)?

---

*Personal Insight: Identify my PER tendency*

---

*"Watch your thoughts, they become words;*
*watch your words, they become actions;*
*watch your actions, they become habits;*
*watch your habits, they become character;*
*watch your character, for it becomes your destiny."*

**~ Author unknown**

At some point, each of us may exhibit a tendency to act in ways that prevent ideal outcomes. This could be triggered by a thought, feeling or action that initiates a *Performance-Eating Rabbit*.

*First: Name It!*

- What is a tendency I have that may get in the way of achieving and supporting a robust outcome?
- What is my PER?

*Second: Identify the trigger*

- What is the trigger that turns on my PER?

*Third: Stop or slow its progress*

- What actions can I take to mitigate or eliminate my PER tendency?
- Who can help, coach or mentor me?
- What is the benefit for me personally if I eliminate this tendency?

## CHAPTER RECAP

- We often come across pesky things that keep us from taking action, finishing what we started, or worse yet, eat at the fabric of who we are.
- *Performance-Eating Rabbits* can be very elusive and sometimes look cute and cuddly on the surface, but then turn out to be the bane of our existence. In the context of improving performance, we simply call these menacing little friends PERs.
- We provide a list of actions to minimize the impact of each PER that includes the following:

| Performance- Eating Rabbit | Actions to Minimize their Impact |
|---|---|
| Political Rabbit | ✓ *Foster a strong trust level within the workforce and leadership.* <br> ✓ *Encourage everyone, regardless of title and role, to constructively and respectfully challenge opinions and ideas.* <br> ✓ *Recognize and reward ideas that make doing the right thing easy and the wrong thing difficult.* <br> ✓ *Eliminate unhealthy competition, especially in critical roles.* |

| | |
|---|---|
| **Hasty Hopper** | ✓ *Keep your strategy simple with performance outcomes that involve both efficiency and effectiveness.*<br>✓ *Leverage their expertise for developing the key predictive indicator for success.*<br>✓ *Apply robust and efficient gap analysis and solution selection prior to execution.* |
| **One-Hit-Wonder Wabbit** | ✓ *Encourage your team to avoid jumping to solutions without first analyzing the causal factors for the current state.*<br>✓ *Implement a structured approach for cause analysis regarding the current state prior to defining the solutions for your initiative.*<br>✓ *Prevent the One-Hit-Wonder Wabbit from dominating conversations with open discussion of the ground truth.*<br>✓ *Listen and encourage the voices in the room who have not yet spoken.* |
| **Bias Bunny** | ✓ *Include everyone in identifying solutions for your strategy.*<br>✓ *Solicit team solutions through an efficient process that is non-threatening.*<br>✓ *Identify the effort and benefit of each solution before deciding on actions.*<br>✓ *Identify early leading indicators or results of the proposed solutions.* |
| **Complacent Bunny** | ✓ *Encourage open and honest conversation – with guidelines for keeping it safe.*<br>✓ *Encourage the complacent participants to openly speak.*<br>✓ *Explain that the risk of staying at "status quo" has significant consequences.*<br>✓ *Include the favorable outcomes they can receive by being fully engaged.* |

| | |
|---|---|
| Culture Rabbit | ✓ Foster a strong positive culture that aligns with the organization's values. <br> ✓ Encourage everyone to challenge solutions that may conflict with their values. <br> ✓ Recognize front-line leaders and workers who demonstrate your counter- culture attributes. This assumes your leadership already demonstrates this! <br> ✓ Eliminate unhealthy competition that would impede trust. <br> ✓ Share stories about the benefits of a new and different desired state. <br> ✓ Clarify the connections between the organization's strategy and those of the individual employee. <br> ✓ Encourage employees to identify their purpose in shaping a different culture. |
| Ledge-Walking Rabbit | ✓ Explain the risk of status quo. <br> ✓ Use a blend of qualitative and quantitative data. <br> ✓ Validate your strategy with internal and external factors. <br> ✓ Share your strategy in detail before you start down the path. <br> ✓ Be ready to engage them in conversation if they start hopping toward a squirrel. |

Congratulations! You reviewed seven *Performance-Eating Rabbits* that can negatively impact your success. We identified key actions to minimize the impact each PER has on achieving successful outcomes.

The next chapter will provide the key tools you can use to mitigate the impact of the *Political Rabbit*.

# CHAPTER 2
## ORGANIZATIONAL TRUTHS

*"To be yourself in a world that is constantly
trying to make you someone else is
the greatest accomplishment."*

**~ Ralf Waldo Emerson**

**How much energy** and resources are wasted on reengineering initiatives, only to find that little (if any) success is achieved? We will spare you the data on successful change initiatives, as it is dismal at best. If you are still reading up to this point, you may be reflecting on a recent project with similar outcomes. So how do we move from defeat to a desired state?

To accomplish a better future, a different approach is required. It demands a fundamental shift in how we think, speak and act. The economy of today requires imagination, exploration, discovery and collaboration; driven by a commitment to make a positive difference in the world.

### Last Lemon on the Lot

Let's be honest - we are sometimes asked to lead, manage and/or support initiatives that fail to hit the mark. The organization is looking to *you* to make the miracle happen. Leadership is counting on *you* to pull everything together, and implement the solutions with all audiences fully engaged and on board. And yes, *you* are expected to execute ahead of schedule and under budget.

The kickoff meeting begins with fanfare, lofty ideals and promises. Beverages and tasty appetizers soothe our initial perception of the future state. We give kudos to the new project leader and team for their commitment and energy to keep the enterprise focused on the tasks at hand that will make the future state a reality.

The charismatic *Political Rabbit* emerges to share the business case for the project. Other leaders in attendance are providing the corporate nod. All the while, they are thinking authentic and practical thoughts like...

- *Whose pet project is this?*
- *What is everyone else in the room thinking or feeling?*
- *Are they kidding? This could never be realized in our lifetime.*
- *How am I going to convince my team to support this?*
- *Do I speak up and challenge the idea?*
- *I will give this initiative three months before it implodes.*

The *Political Rabbit* already anticipated what you are thinking, and frames the solution in a more detailed context as a further attempt to change your perception. At this point, the *Hasty Hoppers* and *Ledge Walking Rabbits* are on board.

In closing, the *Political Rabbit* returns, using a creative idea to solidify your buy-in, by asking you to sign your name to a poster which documents your full devotion and support. The *Complacent Bunnies* lead the way to sign the poster first. This amusing experience is like signing a car dealer's contract of your intent to buy the "Last Lemon on the Lot."

In sharp contrast, we have been privileged to work with leaders who demonstrate BOLD. They are authentic and transparent. They are open to innovative ideas that establish new standards for excellence. They focus on sustainability to achieve continuous improvement which reduces PERs.

A fundamental component we use to begin any improvement initiative is building trust. We believe trust is predicated upon character and competence. Any successful strategy requires a trust level to be sustained and elevated over time. Trust must ultimately transfer through all layers, from the strategy team to the target audience.

Building trust is like managing your bank account. It involves frequent deposits and fewer withdrawals, with continual and vigilant monitoring. Significant trust is achieved when deposits outweigh the withdrawals and your account is positive. Remember that *Political Rabbits* and their cousins thrive in a low trust environment.

> **A fundamental component we use to begin any improvement initiative is building trust.**

*Reader Reflection*

___

- *Describe a recent initiative that had low trust?*
- *What impact did the Political Rabbit have on the outcome?*
- *What triggers told you the initiative had Political Rabbits lurking?*
- *In your opinion, what change was needed for it to be successful?*
- *Were you, (or anyone else) courageous enough to tell stakeholders the truth?*

*Interrogate Reality*

Before creating our client's vision or desired state, we use a simple process called Interrogate Reality. This process allows team members to share and understand the reality, in contrast to the fallacy, about moving in a new direction. We use the terms "ground truth" versus the "official truth" which is referenced in Susan Scott's book *Fierce Conversations*.

For example, if we want to know how a war or conflict is going, we can turn on the news and get the official truth, *"that which is communicated with the approval of an authority or organization."* In this case, that organization would be the television network news agencies. Ground truth, on the other hand, refers to information provided by direct observation (i.e. empirical evidence). If we want to, understand the ground truth, we would interview the Marines and other armed forces who are on the ground in the field of combat. In our situation, we ask what the organizational leaders are saying (official truth) vs. what employees are feeling and experiencing (ground truth).

If the results show there is minimal difference between the official and ground truth, you are fortunate!! If there is a significant difference between official and ground truth, congratulations again -- you now are aware of the issues (perceived or real) which could eat or erode your strategy moving forward. If your view of the present reality is skewed, your future state (along with the strategic actions to get there) is jeopardized.

**Interrogating reality can be the match that lights the fire of open, honest and transparent dialogue.**

When you interrogate reality for the first time, you will be amazed to see the impact it has on developing trust and alignment. We recommend soliciting an authentic and open-minded leader, preferably one who has experienced the ground truth first-hand, to share his or her story before the team starts to complete the exercise. Interrogating reality can be the match that lights the fire of open, honest and transparent dialogue.

Knowing the ground truth allows you and your team to identify counterintuitive actions as part of the strategy to move from current state to desired state. Doing this will help develop trust among the team, and most importantly, identify any PERs that may exist. People who put BOLD into practice understand it is better to succeed long-term with the truth than to temporarily succeed with a lie!

Below is an example of "official truth" versus "ground truth" statements from leaders who were developing a mid-level manager strategy with the objective of attracting and retaining millennial workers.

| Official Truth | Ground Truth |
|---|---|
| We hire, onboard, and set clear expectations | We do not provide enough experiential learning or ownership to keep new hires engaged |
| We have work/life balance | Work out-balances life |
| We have a process in place | The sustainability in the process is not strong |
| We have career paths for mid-level managers | The career paths are limited |
| Our managers are strong mentors | There is evidence that backs this up. |

*Reader Reflection*

- ✓ *What initiative are you working on where you could interrogate reality?*
- ✓ *How are you currently identifying the official and ground truth about your initiative?*
- ✓ *Are you encouraging your team to openly share and contrast the official truth versus ground truth?*

*Reader Practice*

Here is an example of ground truth statements captured in a strategy workshop conducted in an educational setting.

Review each ground truth statement and match the letter of the appropriate *Performance-Eating Rabbits*. Your answer may be different than what we came up with – that's okay, you will be interpreting your answer from your own unique situation.

| Ground Truth Statements | Answer | PER |
|---|---|---|
| 1. Communication issues exist within the Faculty/Staff. | | A. Culture Rabbit |
| 2. Faculty/Staff/Administration are not fully aligned. May be in the same book, but not on the same page. | | B. Hasty Hopper |
| 3. Gossip exists within the organization and is undermining trust. This results in people being guarded in conversation. | | C. One-Hit-Wonder Wabbit |
| 4. All we need is to create a better sense of happiness. | | D. Bias Bunny |
| 5. Issues are not brought up and re-solved between people that have the issues. | | E. Ledge-Walking Rabbit |
| 6. We lack transparent leadership and employee engagement. | | F. Complacent Bunny |
| 7. Our leaders and organization are resistant to change. | | G. Political Rabbit |
| 8. Lower priority tasks limit face to face time within the school day. | | |
| 9. My data shows we need universal support of disciplinary actions. | | |
| 10. Standard expectations for the staff and administration are not com-municated by the principal. | | |

**Answer Key:**

| | | | | |
|---|---|---|---|---|
| 1 = B & C | 2 = E | 3 = A & G | 4 = C | 5 = F |
| 6 = A & G | 7 = A & G | 8 = E | 9 = D | 10 = F |

## CHAPTER RECAP

*Political Rabbits* can de-rail the success of your strategy. You may be condoning their entrance without your knowledge or consent. Once given access, they require constant care and feeding by using valuable time and resources you did not anticipate.

You can minimize *Political Rabbits* early by interrogating reality. Differentiating the official truth from ground truth prior to creating your strategy will disarm them and other PERs. The sponsor and/or team may be blind to their presence.

Interrogating reality will initiate trust with your sponsors and team — Allowing your team to openly identify, share and discuss their ground truth with the rest of the team sets the stage for building trust.

Recognizing *Political Rabbits* is both skill and art. It is not as simple as setting a trap or spraying a certain chemical. They multiply in rapid fashion and blend in with other initiatives that provide them camouflage from being exposed or removed.

Interrogating reality provides guidance to the appropriate actions — Knowing the ground truth will result in taking better strategic actions.

The next chapter will focus on disarming the *Hasty Hopper Rabbit*.

# CHAPTER 3
## PAIN-FREE VISION STATEMENT

*"Our truest life is when we are awake in dreams."*

**~ Henry David Thoreau**

**Each of us** has an image of what our life looks like, and where we will be when we have achieved our life's vision. Ironically, when asked to describe this vision, we either lack the courage, the patience, or the words to share this image in a meaningful manner. We let the *Hasty Hopper* persuade us to quickly share the fastest, safest and most ambiguous vision we can think of. We sometimes fear how others will perceive our life vision; is it too fluffy, too narrow, too broad, too lofty, too hard or too soft? We feel we must find the perfect words to paint this picture of our dreams to ensure that others see it for the gift it truly is.

These same challenges underscore what most feel is the pain and time-draining suffering associated with defining your organization's vision statement. Moreover, the challenges are compounded because organizations experience the insecurities and lack of clarity from the people who shape the vision statement. So, when we receive the invitation to the vision statement meeting (that feels like an invitation from the dentist), we prepare for the days, weeks, months it will take to craft a vision we can live with.

The good news is *we can* breathe life into a vision statement that accurately depicts our ideal organization. The process enables each of us to be inspired and feel we are integral to achieving this vision, without experiencing pain or suffering. Even better, we can harness the need for speed, which the *Hasty Hopper* demands. All you need is twenty minutes and a magic wand to complete a pain free vision statement.

**The good news is *we can* breathe life into a vision statement that accurately depicts our ideal organization.**

*We've Wandered for Forty Days and Forty Nights in the Vision Statement Desert*

We were asked to provide training to a team of medical doctors and nurses to help improve their interdepartmental communication skills. During a break, they were sharing how they had been struggling with developing a vision statement for the newly formed team. They described the challenges they were enduring through the endless meetings, emails and watercooler conversations that had been associated with their progress to date. The look of despair in their eyes (and the hidden cry for help buried in their complaints) prompted us to be BOLD and change the course of our session with them.

We humbly asked them if they were willing to try a new way of creating a vision statement. They skeptically agreed, stating they were willing to try anything to stop what they perceived to be a path of endless suffering. We literally pulled a magic wand (the dollar store variety) out of our bag and asked one of the doctors to wave it over the team and cast the most powerful visioning spell he could possibly conjure up.

The results of this spell, along with a little performance improvement magic from us, enabled the team to articulate the thoughts, feelings and behaviors that would underscore the perfect vision for the team. There was laughter, joy and a sense of ease with the team. After twenty minutes of living the magic, we read aloud the vision statement they had co-created. Their response---a standing ovation!

We've had similar experiences with teams of teachers, summer camp counselors, sales teams, executives, financial professionals, youth groups, manufacturing professionals and even our families. Whether we were creating a vision for the ideal vacation for a handful of our very opinionated and vocal family members, or 150 sales training professionals focused on defining their ideal vision, it worked! All we needed was to be BOLD, trust the power of the magic wand, and the simplicity of defining a pain-free vision statement. The result in each case was a vision statement that resonated with every member of the group along with a sense of amazement that no pain and suffering was necessary.

*Reader Reflection*

- *What fears do you encounter when writing your personal vision statement or developing an organizational vision statement?*
- *Who do you share your personal vision statement with? Why?*
- *What teams or organizations can you work with to practice creating pain-free vision statements?*
- *What would keep you from being BOLD in a vision statement session?*

Leading the development of a pain-free vision statement requires us to capture the *Hasty Hopper* and focus on three essential principles. We must:

- Enable everyone participating to own, silence or simply forget their fears of putting their dreams and voice out on display.
- Do the heavy lifting within the process so that the participants have a pain-free experience.
- Be BOLD in putting our whole-self on display. This includes our thoughts, feelings, beliefs and skills.

The intersection of these three principles with the creative inner voice of each of the participants is where this magical vision-generating process captures the *Hasty Hopper*. Then the beautiful symphony of our organizational dreams comes to life.

Enabling the entire group to own, silence or forget the baggage and fears they brought into the session is an essential first step. Keep in mind, you only need to create this space for the duration of the session. You're good, but even Freud wouldn't be able to untangle the emotional hot mess participants bring with them. This is where we rely on the magic wand.

**You're good, but even Freud wouldn't be able to untangle the emotional hot mess participants bring with them.**

We ask one of the participants to help us make the magic happen. We provide the lucky soul who has volunteered (or been drafted into service) a "special" magic wand. For us, this wand is of the dollar store variety (as we are relatively thrifty) and we like to let our new friend keep it for future use. They are instructed to wave the wand around the room in a manner that only they can. We've had wand wavers anoint each person. We have seen them dance, skip and parade around the room. No matter what their technique, the magical outcome is a playful shift in the room and a subtle excuse for participants to let go of their fears, titles, and distaste for the process. We are now ready to reap the benefits of this magical escape.

The next step is to inform participants that since the magic wand has been waved, their desired state has occurred. We ask them to imagine that when they wake up tomorrow, the vision for their team or organization has become reality. We then ask them the following questions:

- What does this desired state look like?
- What are we doing differently?
- What are the new results realized?

- What are our customers saying about us?
- What is our staff saying about us?
- What are our competitors saying about us?
- How do I feel about being a part of this team?
- How can we measure our new-found success?

We have each team member record their answers to these questions on the Post-It Notes. We have them capture one thought or response per Post-It-Note and ask that they put them to the side as they fill them out. They can provide as many responses as they can imagine (more is definitely better for this activity). We usually play our favorite Neil Diamond song (approximately 3 minutes) on some speakers as they complete the task. It keeps the mood light and gives the team a sense of the duration of the activity without the pressure of a timer or clock.

After participants have provided their responses, we collect the treasures they have provided us. The group can be given a short 15-minute break, or you can have another teaming activity prepared for them to experience while we conduct the rapid microanalysis.

The microanalysis is a blend of open and axial coding of the data. This is qualitative *geek speak,* which means we place the Post-Its on the wall one at a time and we start to group them as we find similarities. We continue this analysis until we have used all the notes, and we freely adjust the groups (or axis) as we receive more information, one Post-It Note at a time. We have conducted this activity for groups of 5 to 150, and have completed this part of the process in 20 minutes.

The process is a lot like when we used to have Valentine's Day parties in grade school. You sat in class and received a variety of cards from your classmates. The cards were a mixed bag of messages that each of us separated on our respective desk by whatever grouping we saw best to use. Some of these cards gave us great joy, some fear, and others just a puzzled expression regarding what it even meant. At the end of the short flurry of what is one of our earliest experiences with microanalysis, we could clearly see the top handful of messages for the day.

Once we have the key axis and the details of each grouping, we BOLD-ly craft the vision statement. We ensure that each major axis is explicitly included in the statement and we leverage the key phrases and language provided by the team to connect these axes into a succinct message. This statement is written or typed so it can be immediately shared with the team. The axes are underlined so the team has visibility into those important elements, and the Post-Its are kept on display so the team can see their input into this magical experience.

**The real magic occurs during the reveal of the newly crafted vision statement.**

The real magic occurs during the reveal of the newly crafted vision statement. We show the team the statement they just co-created in a nearly painless manner and read it aloud to them. We inform them that we can adjust grammar and punctuation as a follow-up action. We then ask them to ensure the vision captures the critical elements and if they can support pursuing it. We sometimes need to make a few subtle adjustments in language to incorporate must-have phrases, but if the analysis is effective, you should require no major changes. You *must* get a sign of agreement from each member of the team. You can have them provide you with a thumbs-up or down, a display of a yes-or-no card, raised hands or whatever method you choose. The key is to get a visible display of agreement.

*Reader practice*

Assemble a group of trusted colleagues, friends or family members to practice creating a vision statement. Follow the steps found in this chapter to understand their collective vision for what an ideal vacation would be. Make sure you have a magic wand and all your needed supplies, then have some fun with this. Upon completion of the session, make sure to get their feedback on how closely aligned the vision statement was to what they felt it should be. Ask them the following questions, and be open and grateful for their input:

- If we were planning a vacation for this group, would you agree that this statement captures our collective vision?
- What went well for you in the session?
- What did not go so well for you in the session?
- What could I do differently next time to make the session better?

Take the feedback to heart and then reflect on the following:

- What did I do well in this session?
- What step in the process do I need to improve on most?
- What was I most comfortable with?
- What will I do differently next time?

After reflecting on the feedback, try the process again. You can either recall the same group with a different topic, or find a new group of trusted peers to explore the vision of their vacations. Or you may do this as part of your volunteer work with smaller teams to continue to refine your skills and increase your comfort with the process.

## CHAPTER RECAP

- This chapter focused on an effective and efficient way to create a vision statement that accurately depicts the desired state of a team while enabling each member of the team to be inspired and feel we are integral to achieving this vision.
- We need to keep the *Hasty Hopper* from persuading us to quickly share the fastest, safest and most ambiguous vision we can think of while we harness the power of its "need for speed."
- We need to be BOLD, trust the power of the magic wand, and the simplicity of defining a pain-free vision statement.
- Analyzing the data from the magic wand exercise requires microanalysis, which is a blend of open and axial coding. This is qualitative *geek speak* that means we place the Post-It Notes on the wall one at a time and we start to group them as we find similarities.
- The real magic occurs during the reveal of the newly crafted vision statement. Be BOLD, stand tall and proud while witnessing the amazement, satisfaction and looks of relief from the team.

While this chapter mitigated the *Hasty Hopper* by ensuring that a pain-free vision statement was developed, the vision is simply a dream until the team can take action and move it toward their desired state. The following chapter will help you identify where the *One-Hit-Wonder Wabbit* has placed barriers in the way and will provide a great tool to keep it from convincing you and your team that there is only one road to success.

# CHAPTER 4
# TRAPPING THE ONE-HIT-WONDER WABBIT

*"Do the thing you think you cannot do."*

**~ Eleanor Roosevelt**

**There will come** a time when counterintuitive thinking will benefit the outcomes you are striving to achieve. We must refuse the "suckers' choice" of being an order taker and BOLD-ly do what you know in your heart, mind and soul ultimately will win the day!

In chapter two we discussed interrogating reality to clarify the ground truth about circumstances to expose *Political Rabbits*. In chapter three we mitigated the *Hasty Hopper* by developing a pain free vision statement. You may be feeling, at this point, you have a clear path moving forward. Unfortunately, there are other cousins in the PER family that still pose an impediment to your success. The *One-Hit-Wonder Wabbit* now springs into action as you start to identify and implement your solutions.

## My Teenager is Failing

Throughout life we all face difficult circumstances. How we listen, speak and act on those difficult situations speaks volumes about who we are as a person. The ground truth is that we tend to anxiously jump to solutions without understanding the issue or the factors causing the situation in the first place. We become further frustrated when we select a solution, only to find the outcome did not correct the problem or made it worse.

**We tend to anxiously jump to solutions without understanding the issue or the factors causing the situation in the first place.**

If you are a parent of teenagers, you deserve a medal of honor for accepting the daunting task of raising and mentoring your son or daughter. On their journey to adulthood, you may have been carefully guiding and anticipating the day your teen attends a prestigious university and pursues a degree that aligns with their dream. Up to this point, your teen is achieving the exceptional grades necessary for a good chance to attend the university of their choice. You come home from a brutal day in the workplace only to find a letter from their high school stating *your teenager is failing!*

*What will you do?*

Will you step back and analyze the causal factors of the issue, or will you jump to a solution? If we are honest, we may do the latter and assume the problem is "my teenager," even though they performed consistently well in the past.

What if we allowed BOLD to take over our thinking and resisted the temptation to ground our teenager from any privileges for life? What if you were open to apply a new way of thinking about the issue? What questions would you ask yourself and your teen before considering the solution, and prevent the *One-Hit-Wonder Wabbit* from eroding the relationship between you and your teen? What if you considered other factors that are causing the issue?

Note: In the example above, you may be wondering what caused the student's apparent failure. The actual problem was with the software used to capture and report test scores. It was proven to be faulty, and eventually new corrected scores were issued. Hence, no grounding needed and the teenager was able keep their cell phone.

*Reader Reflection*

- *What additional factors are preventing your teenager or enterprise from unleashing greatness?*
- *When have you observed "Worthy Performance" of a family member, team or company?*
  - O *What characteristics or factors supported what you observed?*
- *Recall a project where the One-Hit-Wonder Wabbit won the day and got their way?*
  - O *What was the outcome?*
- *Describe a time when you pro-actively identified causal factors before identifying solutions?*
  - O *How did it turn out? What tools did you choose?*

Performing a thorough analysis of causal factors incorporates a level of critical systems thinking. It involves asking powerful questions about environmental and individual factors.

When we get the scent of a lurking *One-Hit-Wonder Wabbit*, we leverage a simple and systematic tool called Rapid Gap Analysis (RGA). Conducting an RGA is an efficient and effective method to identify multiple causal factors that could be impacting (positively or negatively) your desired outcome. If we are creating an organizational strategy, we conduct the Rapid Gap Analysis after interrogating reality and developing the Pain-Free Vision statement.

*Tools/Principles of the Chapter*

| Information | Instrumentation | Motivation | |
|---|---|---|---|
| **DATA** | **INSTRUMENTS** | **INCENTIVES** | |
| • Data and Information Metrics<br>• Communication and Feedback | • Tools<br>• Resources<br>• Work environment | • Incentives<br>• Consequences<br>• Rewards | Rooted in the Environment/ Organization |
| **KNOWLEDGE** | **CAPACITY** | **MOTIVES** | |
| • Skills<br>• Knowledge<br>• Behavior | • Individual capacity | • Recognition<br>• Motivation<br>• Expectations | Rooted in the Individual Worker |

Thomas Gilbert
Fundamentals of Human Performance Technology
Published by ISPI 2010

Thomas Gilbert is credited for establishing the Behavioral Engineering Model. In the late 1970s he suggested methods for engineering the ideal (or worthy) performance. Through the 1980s the focus on performance flourished. In the 1990s, organizations began to recognize the value of Performance Technology because of its link to business goals - the interventions suggested in the analysis were tied back to measures that mattered. Many performance improvement practitioners today may refer to it as the Six Cell model. This model simplifies causal factors and enforcers that are rooted in the environment, as well as factors that are rooted in the individual worker.

These performance factors fall into the following six categories:

- Data, information, and feedback
- Environmental support, resources, and tools
- Consequences, incentives or rewards
- Skills and knowledge
- Individual capacity
- Motives and expectations

These are the categories adopted by the International Society for Performance Improvement (ISPI). Other authors cite anywhere from three to eleven categories, but the principle remains the same; multiple factors support worthy performance and also cause performance problems (areas for improvement). Once these causes are identified, appropriate solutions can be designed and implemented to mitigate the performance gap and unleash exceptional performance. We use the principles of Gilbert's six cell to conduct a process we developed called the Rapid Gap Analysis.

### Conducting a Rapid Gap Analysis (RGA)

Facilitating our RGA session is relatively easy. Using a set of targeted powerful questions, responses will uncover specific factors causing the problem, or preventing your current solutions from working. The RGA also illuminates factors that can support the success of your initiative. In addition, you also receive the gift of a qualitative rating for each of the six cell categories.

**Facilitating our RGA session is relatively easy.**

The materials you will need are simply a flip chart and colored markers. We typically use red, orange (in place of yellow for visibility) and green markers for each table. We recommend having table groups of 4-6 participants to enhance dialog and discussion.

Identify and invite individuals close to the issue to attend the one hour RGA meeting. This includes subject matter experts (SMEs); which, as we have observed, could also mean "someone management elected." The important thing is to select people who work closely with the issue. You can also invite any *One-Hit Wonder Rabbits* who believe the team doesn't have to do any more "analysis-paralysis" since their solution will fix the issue. Consider inviting any *Hasty Hoppers* who are interested in seeing a holistic process completed in less than an hour.

We encourage you to review the questions we provided in the

RGA job aid before the session. It includes probing questions within each of the six cells to initiate discussion at each table. Go ahead and modify and add your own questions that may be more specific to the issue you are working on. This best practice allows more clarity on specific gaps and makes it easier for your audience to "get it done!"

*RGA Job Aid -Targeted Questions for Environmental Factors*

| Environmental Factors | | |
|---|---|---|
| **DATA** | **Instruments** | **Incentives** |
| What are expectations of the workforce (target audience)?<br><br>Are the workforce expectations clear and measurable?<br><br>Where do individuals go to find answers for performing their work? Does the support help or hinder their success?<br><br>What metrics and/ or feedback is used to monitor worker performance?<br><br>Are your current metrics leading or lagging indicators?<br><br>What are some of the ways you provide the high-level outcomes?<br><br>What documents (or information) support their performance? | What word or phrase would you use to indicate the current work environment?<br><br>Are departments adequately staffed to perform the work?<br><br>What tools or instruments help or hinder completion of the work?<br><br>Are the procedures and processes for completing the work efficient and effective?<br><br>What actions establish the perfect environment for your workforce?<br><br>Can the worker/team realistically complete the required tasks (work) in the time allotted? | What are the rewards for achieving exceptional performance?<br><br>What is the perception of the incentive system?<br><br>Does the workforce know the incentives exist?<br><br>What consequences are in place for poor performance? Are they used?<br><br>Does the workforce know the consequences for poor performance exist?<br><br>What are the career advancement opportunities for an exemplar performer?<br><br>How is success of the incentive system measured? |

©Performance Journey Partners, LLC

*RGA Job Aid - Targeted Questions for Individual Worker Factors*

| Individual Worker Factors | | |
|---|---|---|
| **Knowledge** | **Capacity** | **Motives** |
| How is the target audience trained to perform their role? Is it effective and/or efficient?<br><br>How is the target audience trained to report and correct potential mistakes in the work?<br><br>What knowledge and skills are critical for the performer to deliver high quality service or results?<br><br>What are the key behaviors that support the performance you desire?<br><br>Does your workforce demonstrate those behaviors? | What standard selection criteria is used to hire a team member in this role?<br><br>How do typical workers feel at the end of their shift or work experience?<br><br>What specific experiences and attributes do you look for in selecting a job candidate?<br><br>How does the expected work align to the department's mission and vision?<br><br>What are the current employee retention metrics for this role? | How would you rate the current motivation of the team members?<br><br>How do team members motivate each other to "be on their game"?<br><br>How do they stay motivated to provide the exceptional service you provide?<br><br>What de-railers exist that could impair team motivation?<br><br>What word describes a worker's attitude? |

©Performance Journey Partners, LLC

When your audience arrives, provide a brief introduction of the RGA purpose. Encourage participants to think in a more holistic and open minded way, identifying potential causes for the issue at hand. Appoint a table leader and scribe for each table. The table leader is responsible for initiating discussion and sharing their insights at the end of the activity. The scribe captures their group's feedback and consensus rating of the gap severity for each cell on their flip chart. This allows each table group to manage their own outcomes.

Provide each participant the RGA Job Aid using questions you revised (or review our questions found in Chapter 10). Tell participants they do not have to answer each question in the job aid, as it is intended to be used as a guideline to start discussion. The *Hasty Hopper* in the room will give you a "thumbs up" (as they appreciate the efficiency of the process). Allow each table group 30 minutes to complete the exercise. Next, ask each table leader to initiate discussion with their table group using the list of questions. The scribe at each table will capture the responses onto a flip chart. When they have identified several factors in each cell, the table leader asks them to color code each six-cell box to indicate the severity of the gap (Major = red, Moderate = orange and Minor = green).

- Red indicates major gaps that *will* impede the desired outcome.
- Orange indicates moderate gaps that *could* impede the desired outcome.
- Green indicates few or no gaps, with little to no impact to the desired outcome.

After each table leader shares their feedback, we encourage the entire room to "applaud wildly." We also like to verbally recognize the table leader and scribe for their heroic work. At this point we have participants take a short break. We take their flip charts and transfer their data into a six-cell template. It's easy to identify the common gaps and themes from each table group. We then share the summary of factors and their ratings with all table groups.

Congrats! Your team has identified the causal factors for the

**Your team has identified the causal factors for the problem; it now becomes easier to identify solutions.** problem; it now becomes easier to identify solutions. Hopefully, the *One-Hit Wonder Wabbit* has realized that his solution will not achieve the success your team is counting on. The *Political Rabbit* is surprised with meaningful data. The *Hasty Hopper* is asking if they can facilitate this session with their team in the future.

*Reader Reflection*

- *What additional questions would you use if you were doing an RGA at work?*
- *What additional questions would you use if you were doing an RGA at home?*
- *What additional questions would you use if you were doing an RGA in your community?*

*Reader Practice*

Following is an RGA completed at a strategy development session for mid-level managers to attract and retain millennial workers.

*Instructions*: Review the results and identify the causal factors that present major roadblocks to achieving success.

| Major Gaps |
| Moderate Gaps |
| Few or None |

| Information | Instrumentation | Motivation |
|---|---|---|
| **DATA** | **INSTRUMENTS/ RESOURCES** | **INCENTIVES** |
| • Inconsistent systems of records<br>• Development and expectations are not aligned<br>• Individual performance not connected to org performance<br>• Data not being used<br>• Focus is more on lagging measures<br>• Meetings are not efficient | • Current processes don't align to bigger picture<br>• Reactive vs proactive<br>• Traditional environment is 'old school'<br>• We don't invest in the right tools to meet the work capacity | • Bonus (annual)<br>• Merit increase<br>• Peer to peer recognition programs<br>• Salary not matching work load<br>• Work/life flexibility jeopardized |
| **KNOWLEDGE** | **CAPACITY** | **MOTIVES** |
| • Some Online / e-learning; not engaging<br>• Some mentoring<br>• No measurement of effectiveness | • Slow to make hiring decisions<br>• Recruiting to core competencies<br>• High retention of mid-managers | • There are international opportunities for high performers<br>• High engagement<br>• Not clear how opportunities are awarded |

©Performance Journey Partners, LLC

- *What are the major causal factors that would prevent the desired state from occurring?*
- *Which cell has few or no gaps?*
- *How does the RGA tool minimize the One Hit Wonder Wabbit?*

Imagine yourself collaborating with a leader and their team in the following scenario:

The leader has decided to improve their current state. They contact you because they believe you are the *One-Hit-Wonder Wabbit* with -- you guessed it! -- the one solution they believe will revolutionize their process and put them at the top, in terms of outcomes and status within the industry.

You listen for fifteen minutes as the team passionately shares their story about the initiative (which seems more like fifteen hours). They pro-actively benchmarked competitors and believed once this one solution was implemented, it would correct all the issues, inspire the organization, and achieve the "Best Practice" status from internal and external standards. At this point you can serve as the "Order Taker" -- provide the single solution and lose this to the *One-Hit-Wonder Wabbit* mindset. You realize, however, that the following issues exist:

- Your success is predicated on the team's success.
- You know that problems typically have multiple causes, which require blended solutions.
- The consequence of failure is not an option.
- You want to be BOLD and define new standards for excellence.

So, you seize the opportunity to be BOLD (open minded and leading with courage and humility), to keep them in the conversation without bursting their bubble! You re-state what you heard, and then ask for permission to relate a different story about what *could* happen if they allowed you to spend forty-five minutes with the team completing the RGA process.

They agree to proceed, and in less than one hour (using the RGA process), they identified multiple factors that were preventing their desired state. What you hypothesized was true! The one solution may have helped, but would not have fully achieved their desired outcome. The RGA identified additional causal factors that the single solution (initially proposed), would not have addressed.

After the meeting, the team and sponsor thank you for helping them see the bigger picture and for investing in their success. You have won the battle over the *One-Hit-Wonder Wabbit* and helped the leader avoid potential failure. You also prevented them from becoming a *Ledge Walking Rabbit*.

## Chapter Recap

- This chapter focused on the importance of preventing the *One-Hit-Wonder Wabbit* with BOLD thinking and the help of the Rapid Gap Analysis to understand the causal factors.
- The RGA identifies causal factors in the environment, which include: data, information, instruments, incentives and consequences. The RGA also identifies factors attributed to individual repertory (knowledge, skill, individual capacity and internal motivation). Segmenting these causal factors help you and your organization target solutions that minimize the negative impact, and stops the *One-Hit-Wonder Wabbit* from taking over.
- Conducting a Rapid Gap Analysis provides targeted guidance on selecting holistic solutions. Knowing the multiple

causal factors will assist you and your team in identifying blended solutions that enable better outcomes.

- The RGA provides cost avoidance in time and effort, not to mention investing in solutions that don't deliver desired results for you or your enterprise.

**Preventing the *One-Hit-Wonder Wabbit* is key to ensuring that the solutions fix the big issues.**

Preventing the *One-Hit-Wonder Wabbit* is key to ensuring that the solutions fix the big issues. The next chapter will allow you to focus on generating the right solutions to eliminate or minimize actions of the *Bias Bunny* and other PERs.

# CHAPTER 5
## SPEED DATING FOR SOLUTIONS

*"You are either part of the solution*
*or part of the problem."*

**~ Eldridge Cleaver**

**Leaders and problem-solvers** can appear calm, cool and seemingly open to resolving organizational challenges. However, they may have a deep-seated aversion when it comes to trying new and innovative solutions to emerging problems. They may lose sight of the real issue, and purely rely on their previous success to quickly shift the focus off them and their team.

In this fast-paced world, there are times when we are told to accept, adopt, or support initiatives we believe are not right or ethical. If we are authentic with ourselves, we will fight back the urge to be an order taker. Setting new paths for excellence -- combined with an efficient process to identify right solutions -- is critical in every industry and walk of life.

> **There are times when we are told to accept, adopt, or support initiatives we believe are not right or ethical.**

Would you believe it is possible to identify and prioritize up to 150 solutions in thirty minutes? If not, it's time to open your mind to new possibilities and simply be amazed!

In this chapter, we introduce a method to harness the creative and collaborative spirit of the team, while establishing clear organizational effort and benefit. This process enables you to engage

the innovative spirit of the team. It engages people to quickly identify solutions while vetting their merits in a rapid fashion. The ge-
nius who provided inspiration for this activity is Sivasailam "Thiagi"
Thiagarajan. He is acknowledged as the world's foremost authority
on interactive learning. His innovative thinking prompted the cre-
ation of Speed Dating for Solutions, which mitigates the *Bias Bunny*
as well as the *One-Hit-Wonder Wabbit.*

## Reader Reflection

- *How do you currently approach solutions? Is it a formal or informal process?*
- *What challenges do you encounter when identifying solutions?*
- *What is your current success rate of recommending solutions that achieve desired results?*

## Tools/Principles of the Chapter

### 21 Activity – Speed Dating for Solutions

We named this process using a "speed dating" metaphor since it is
similar to the process followed in a speed dating event. The key difference is you are looking for solutions, not for romantic love! However,
there is one common element between speed dating for solutions and
the actual practice of speed dating. You may fall in love... with this tool.
Try it and see for yourself and watch out for cupid.

Twenty-one represents the perfect score for an idea generated
using this tool. The activity itself can be completed in 30 minutes if
you use this process. This simple and impactful exercise will clear
the garden path of PERs, especially the *Bias Bunny.*

First, invite a group of participants who are seeking solutions to
an issue that is keeping them up at night, or worse, preventing their

strategy from achieving a successful lift-off.

Note: We encourage inviting as many people as possible in generating solutions. It's a simple equation, the more participants = more solutions generated. We have facilitated this activity with over 150 participants. It becomes a speed dating frenzy! To further build the excitement, we do this activity not in a conference room, but in their favorite location. We once had the opportunity to facilitate this activity while gazing at the Golden Gate Bridge in San Francisco. The location you choose, combined with the 21 activity, will make it memorable! We strongly suggest you purchase a train whistle to signal the beginning and conclusion for each of the seven rounds.

After describing the purpose of the tool, we provide the 21 Activity handout and review instructions for the exercise. We then ask each participant to write down their idea/solution that will fix the issue or eliminate the cause for a given problem.

After everyone has recorded their idea, we ask them to exchange it with someone else in the room. This step is *critical* to mitigate the *Bias Bunny*. If you are the participant, the solution you wrote down is now gifted to someone else. You also are the recipient of a solution from another participant. The gift you have **A gift is not a gift until it is given and received** received is now *your* solution for the rest of the exercise. Please thank your colleague for the gift, as a gift is not a gift until it is given and received...mind your manners!

Tell everyone to form groups of three and give instructions on how to dialog and score each idea. To make it easy, we show by example how a round is played. Have fun with this and keep it simple. In groups of three, each person quickly shares their idea. Then the group will discuss each of the solutions and score each idea using a maximum of 3 points for the best idea, 2 points for the second best and 1 point for the remaining idea. Each person then records their score in Round 1 of your handout. Don't worry if there is a group of 4; the fourth best idea also gets 1 point. After scoring the ideas, ask them to estimate the amount of effort and benefit (using Low, Moderate or High) and again record the results for your idea under the appropriate Effort/Benefit column for the specific round.

Once everyone has finished the first round, pull out your trusty train whistle and blow loudly! Tell participants to connect with two new people and begin the round two. The pace of the exercise gets faster each round as networking ideas with others gains momentum. Continue each round in the same fashion until the group has completed seven rounds. Depending on the size of the group, you may choose to play fewer rounds.

After all rounds are completed, tell participants to total up the score for their idea and average their Effort and Benefit rating at the bottom of the activity sheet. To celebrate and keep momentum going, we ask participants to share their idea with the highest scores. (Encourage wild applause!) Then ask who gave them the gift of the great solution. Doing this simple recognition builds trust and collaboration.

A completed 21 Activity is shown here:

## 21 ACTIVITY – SPEED DATING FOR SOLUTIONS

*This activity will generate, analyze, and prioritize ideas on a given topic using collaborative inquiry.*

### Step 1: Capture your idea.

Take a minute to generate a solution for achieving our desired state.

---

**Idea/Solution:** *Idea for increasing knowledge of work policies – create a site for our team where we can have folders for activities we perform and upload templates, completed examples, and job aides. This will give us access to best practices, reduce variance, and help new employees understand what completed work looks like.*

---

## Step 2: Exchange idea w/someone else.

After exchanging your idea, take a moment to ensure you understand the solution you now hold. Note: You will retain this new solution throughout each scoring activity during step 3.

## Step 3: Participate in scoring activity.

Share and discuss the idea you have with two fellow colleagues. Rate/score each idea for this round using a maximum of **3 points for the best idea, 2 points for the second-best idea and 1 point for remaining idea(s)** and record the score of this idea in the box below. If there is a group of 4; the fourth best idea also gets 1 point.

Rate and record the level of effort and benefit for each idea (**H**=High, **M**=Moderate, **L**=Low) in the box below.

After the scoring for the round is complete, seek out two new people and repeat the process.

| | **Idea Score** (3/2/1) | **Effort** (H/M/L) | **Benefit** (H/M/L) |
|---|---|---|---|
| Round 1 | 3 | H | H |
| Round 2 | 2 | M | H |
| Round 3 | 3 | H | M |
| Round 4 | 3 | M | H |
| Round 5 | 2 | M | H |
| Round 6 | 2 | M | M |
| Round 7 | 3 | H | H |
| | Total: 18 | Avg. M/H | Avg. H |

©Performance Journey Partners, LLC

At this point we give participants a short break while we record each solution into a simple template that represents their score, effort and benefit ratings. We call it the *reveal*.

When participants return from break, we share the results of the activity. The *reveal* allows participants to take a strategic look at the solutions that have a low effort, high benefit, and with the highest score. At the same time, we look at solutions which may not have received the highest score, yet may have the lowest effort and highest benefit. Since speed dating is not an Olympic sport, you get no extra credit for tackling the most difficult solution first or ever!

**The *Bias Bunny, One-Hit-Wonder Wabbit and Political Rabbits* will be left powerless to take credit for their idea.**

Moving to action becomes simple. The facilitator asks, "Who is passionate about leading solution X?" and "Who wants to spearhead solution Y?" If you don't get an immediate volunteer, find the brave souls who make eye contact with you and BOLD-ly put them on the spot!

The *Bias Bunny, One-Hit-Wonder Wabbit and Political Rabbits* will be left powerless to take credit for their idea. The *Culture Bunny* will likely wonder *"What just happened?"* and the *Hasty Hoppers*, who represent overworked leaders, will be warming up to your method of harvesting solutions so quickly.

The solutions you obtain from this activity will achieve the following:

- Allow everyone to express their solution while minimizing bias
- Identify solutions that may be similar
- Foster trust among the participants
- Gain consensus of the best solutions

We hope by now you're thinking, *"When and where can I use*

*speed dating with my team, a committee, or even with my in-laws (out-laws) to identify solutions for next year's summer vacation!"*

## CHAPTER RECAP

- Arriving at the right set of solutions for a performance issue can be difficult and time consuming.
- There are times when our solution is the right solution. But if we are authentic with ourselves, we must admit there are also times when we know the solution on the table is not right or ethical.
- Using the 21 Activity tool makes it possible to identify, evaluate, prioritize and determine the effort, benefit and risk of solutions in thirty minutes.
- The 21 Activity mitigates the *Bias Bunny,* the *One-Hit-Wonder Wabbit* and *Political Rabbit.*

So, we have solutions identified and have remained free from PERs derailing our process. However, we have not moved into implementing our solutions. The next chapter tackles how to handle the *Complacent Bunny.* Read on with courage!

# CHAPTER 6
## THE STRATEGIC F WORD

*"If the ladder is not leaning against the right wall, every step we take just gets us to the wrong place faster."*

**~ Stephen R. Covey**

**When working on** the strategic elements of performance improvement, we find people struggling with the foulest and most dreaded F word we face in public settings…… your mom would be horrified by what you are thinking…. The F word is feelings.

Many times, in our professional and personal lives, we have a picture of perfection in mind. We can see it, feel it, smell it, and hear it. Sometimes we can even taste the success of achieving our strategic vision. The problem is, we often neglect to ensure that this vision (and the actions associated with achieving it) are aligned to the reality of who we are today (along with the underlying thoughts and feelings that will drive us). We sense the crushing wave of feelings associated with realizing our strategic vision is unattainable or simply not aligned with our organization. Even worse, we can become complacent and accept *status quo* as better than experiencing our potential. We align our strategic vision and adjust our course to address current realities. We run the risk of falling victim to the *Complacent Bunny*.

The *Complacent Bunny* has two key tricks in its bag that we need to be aware of and address head-on. The first trick is a magic powder that blinds us from truly understanding the realities of our organizations, teams, and the external environment within which they operate. The second trick forces us to ignore the underlying thoughts and feelings of our organizations concerning our strategies. Both tricks are equally damaging to our success, and at the same time, are equally as easy to negate by BOLD-ly using a modified SWOT analysis and a Culture Pulse.

## SSDD (Same Stuff Different Day)

We were running an in-service for the faculty and staff of a local elementary school. The teams were busy setting their goals for the upcoming year, telling stories of their summer fun, and reminiscing about successes and challenges of previous school years and the students that inspire them (or make them question their choice of profession). As we began the strategy summary for the whole team, something changed. The fun collaborative feeling in the room began to shift and feel like one of those awkward meetings where the presenter either has a huge coffee stain on their shirt or a booger hanging from their nose. Everyone sees it, but nobody says anything. It was a dare to be BOLD moment, and a great opportunity to see if the *Complacent Bunnies* were up to one of their tricks.

**Everyone sees it, but nobody says anything.**

The modified SWOT analysis and Culture Pulse quickly revealed a handful of archaic policies, a perceived lack of empowerment, and an underlying fear of challenge had already derailed each of the goals being presented. The team had seen this before and was going to chalk the day up as a mostly fun session that was well intended, but not one that would enable their strategic vision to be realized in the upcoming school year and beyond. But, since the team could safely share their thoughts and feelings through the culture pulse, they quantitatively demonstrated the misalignment of their strategy through the modified SWOT. The team refined their goals to drive the results they envisioned. Additionally, each member of the faculty felt understood, included and empowered.

*Reader Reflection*
___

- *Recall a project where your strategies didn't align to the current strengths and weakness of your team.*
  - ○ *What were the outcomes?*
  - ○ *When did you realize the misalignment?*
  - ○ *Who identified the challenges and how were they perceived?*
- *What barriers prevent you from addressing the thoughts and feelings of your team?*
- *Recall a recent project where the thoughts and feelings of the team positively impacted their outcomes.*
  - ○ *How did you know the thoughts and feelings were addressed?*
  - ○ *What are the top three to five things that resulted from addressing the thoughts and feelings?*

*Tools/Principles of the Chapter*
___

*Modified SWOT (Strength, Weakness, Opportunity, Threats)*

The purpose of the Modified SWOT is to ensure that your strategies and goals are aligned with your current state capabilities and the pressing things in your environment. This will ensure you are really climbing the ladder of success and not the long ladder to nowhere. You need to quantitatively and qualitatively analyze both the internal strengths and weaknesses of the team, as well as their external opportunities and threats. This analysis can then be safely and succinctly discussed and actioned by the team in the moment.

The quantitative element and rapid action is how our approach differs from the traditional SWOT. Many practitioners collect the list of strengths and so on, and proudly display them on the wall as a work of art, worthy of being compared to masterpieces like the *Mona Lisa* or *The Birth of Venus*. Once the team has viewed and acknowledged the freshly painted SWOT, they complacently nod their heads and move on with no practical use for what they have just created. If we let this happen, we have fallen prey to the *Complacent Bunny*.

Instead, we leverage a simple approach taught to most MBA students by generating internal factor evaluation matrixes (IFE), and external factor evaluation matrixes (EFE). We can then move on to create a clear map of how strategies and goals align, and where they don't. WARNING: This section actually requires some math. We know that this is the worst 4-letter word some of you know, but we have provided some straightforward directions and examples to ease the pain. We promise no fancy new math is being used.

The first step is to ask the team to share what they feel are the strengths, weaknesses, opportunities and threats for their team (in the context of the vision they are pursuing). This portion of the SWOT shouldn't take any more than five minutes. Capture the team's responses on a flip chart or other tool, where they can then see them and help them fight the urge to overthink the activity. Once you have 4-7 responses in each SWOT category, then move the team to the next category. When you have the strengths, weaknesses and opportunities listed, then quickly begin to collect the additional data needed to complete the IFE and EFE matrixes.

## Internal Factor Evaluation (IFE)

The IFE matrix compares the internal strengths and weaknesses of the team and provides a numeric score that shows the overall health of the team and their ability to either capitalize on their opportunities, or protect themselves from their threats. Start by listing the strengths and weaknesses in the table below. You can get the remaining data needed for this analysis by asking two questions about each strength and weakness listed.

The first question is, which of the strengths and weaknesses are most important to the team? Ask them to pick the top three strengths and weaknesses from the list they feel are most impactful to the team. You can have the team place tally marks or stickers on the list you provide, or use an automated polling tool to capture the information. Calculate the percentage of responses for each by dividing the total number of responses for each strength and weakness by the total number of potential responses. The total number of potential responses is calculated by multiplying the number of participants by six.

Record the data in Column B of the following table, and be aware that these entries will be decimals and should add up to 1.0 if you have done the math right.

The second question is to understand just how significant each strength or weakness item is to the team. You use a scale from one to four to capture this information. The following is the scale:

1. Major weakness
2. Minor Weakness
3. Minor Strength
4. Major Strength.

You can use a polling tool, response cards or a paper scorecard to record each team member's response. The key is to use a tool that allows each person to respond without speaking, debating or arguing. After the responses are received, all you need is the average score for each strength and weakness, and enter the average into column C in the following table.

| A | B | C | D |
|---|---|---|---|
| Critical Success Factors | Weight | Rating | Weighted Score |
| Strengths | | | |
| | | | |
| | | | |
| | | | |
| Weakness | | | |
| | | | |
| | | | |
| | | | |
| TOTAL | | | |

To complete the IFE, you simply need to multiply columns B and C together and record the answer in Column D. Once you have done this for each strength and weakness, add up all the responses in column D. The sum of responses in column D will be between 1 and 4 and should be reported to include one decimal place (i.e. 2.5, 1.2 etc.). This number provides you with the overall internal health of the team.

Your final step in preparing the IFE for discussion with the team is to perform the qualitative analysis of the data. This analysis is a ton easier than the fun-filled math refresher you just read about. First, articulate what the IFE score means to the team. If your final score is below 2.0, then your strategies and goals need to enhance the strengths of the team and eliminate their weaknesses. If you don't, then the probability of achieving your desired state is not very good. If the score is above a 2.0, then your strengths outweigh your weaknesses, and your strategies should directly focus on the opportunities and threats you have identified. The closer to 4.0 the team is, the stronger they are.

Next share the specifics of where the team is strong and where it is not. Column D of the table shows a weighted score for each strength and weakness and provides the team the ability to see and discuss the specific items that either make them great, or are causing them to be very ineffective. Your responsibility is to summarize these findings, share them with the team and provide a safe and open forum for a brief discussion. Make sure any additional goals or adjustments to defined strategies are recorded. Here's an example of an IFE summary.

| A | B | C | D |
|---|---|---|---|
| Critical Success Factors | Weight | Rating | Weighted Score |
| **Strengths** | | | |
| Knowledge of Patients | 0.01 | 2 | 0.03 |
| Experience | 0.10 | 3.3 | 0.33 |
| Commitment | 0.09 | 3.4 | 0.30 |
| Passion for work | 0.11 | 3 | 0.33 |
| Knowledge of manufacturing process | 0.09 | 3 | 0.28 |
| Closer to ground truth | 0.03 | 2.5 | 0.07 |
| **Weakness** | | | |
| Pulse on our customers | 0.04 | 1.5 | 0.06 |
| Prioritization (lack of) | 0.11 | 1.3 | 0.15 |
| Courage to say no – focus on priorities | 0.07 | 1.6 | 0.11 |
| Decisive decision making | 0.07 | 1.7 | 0.13 |
| Making a decision stick & sustain | 0.07 | 1.6 | 0.12 |
| Bureaucracy | 0.11 | 1.2 | 0.13 |
| Sole source knowledge centrality | 0.02 | 1.7 | 0.04 |
| Contingent labor strategy | 0.08 | 1.5 | 0.12 |
| **TOTAL** | **1** | | **2.2** |

*External Factor Evaluation (EFE)*

The EFE matrix compares the external opportunities and threats of the team and provides a numeric score that highlights where the team needs to prioritize their strategies and goals. Start by entering the opportunities and strengths to column A of the table below. You can get the remaining data needed for this analysis by asking two questions about each opportunity and threat listed. Like the IFE, the first question is, which of the opportunities and threats are most important to the team?

Ask them to pick the top three opportunities and threats from the list which they feel are most impactful to the team. Have the team place tally marks or stickers on the list you provide or use an automated polling tool to capture the information. Calculate the percentage of responses for each by dividing the total number of responses for each strength and weakness by the total number of potential responses. The total number of potential responses is calculated by multiplying the number of participants by six. Record the data in Column B of the following table and be aware that these entries will be decimals and should add up to 1.0 if you have done the math right.

The second question to ask is, how well are the organization's current strategies and goals addressing the identified opportunities and threats? Use a scale from one to four to capture this information:

1. Poor
2. Average
3. Above Average
4. Superior

You can use a polling tool, response cards or a paper scorecard to record each team member's response. The key is to use a tool that allows each person to respond without speaking, debating or arguing. After the responses are received, all you need is the average score for each opportunity and threat and enter the average into column C in the following table.

| A | B | C | D |
|---|---|---|---|
| Critical Success Factors | Weight | Rating | Weighted Score |
| Opportunities | | | |
| | | | |
| | | | |
| | | | |
| Threats | | | |
| | | | |
| | | | |
| | | | |
| TOTAL | | | |

To complete the EFE, you simply need to multiply columns B and C together and record the answer in Column D. Once you have done this for each opportunity and threat, add up all the responses in column D. The sum of responses in column D will be between 1 and 4 and should be reported to include one decimal place (i.e. 2.5, 1.2 etc.). This number provides you with direction on where the team should focus their strategies.

Your next step in preparing the EFE for discussion with the team is to perform the qualitative analysis of the data. First, articulate what the EFE score means to the team. If your final score is below 2.0, then your strategies and goals need to focus on defending the organization from the threats that were identified. If you don't, the team may never get the chance to realize the potential benefits of their identified opportunities. If the score is above a 2.0, then your opportunities outweigh their weaknesses and their strategies should directly focus on the opportunities and simply keep an eye on the threats. The closer to 4.0 the score is, the less likely their strategies will be derailed by their threats.

Now you will be able to share the specifics of which opportunities and threats should be top priorities for the team. Column D of the table shows a weighted score for each opportunity and threat. It then provides the team the ability to see and discuss the specific items that could be either hugely beneficial or most damaging. Your responsibility is to summarize these findings, share it with the team, and provide a safe and open forum for a brief discussion. Make sure any additional adjustments to defined strategies and goals are recorded. Here's an example of an EFE summary.

| A<br>Critical Success Factors | B<br>Weight | C<br>Rating | D<br>Weighted Score |
|---|---|---|---|
| **Opportunities** | | | |
| Learning from millennial | 0.13 | 1.7 | 0.22 |
| Form mutually beneficial partnership to drive innovation | 0.17 | 1.8 | 0.31 |
| Increase the ability to attract millennials | 0.20 | 1.8 | 0.36 |
| Educate midlevel managers to share their knowledge and experience | 0.13 | 1.8 | 0.23 |
| Redefine relevant retention targets for millennials | 0.08 | 1.5 | 0.12 |
| **Threats** | | | |
| High Turnover (cost) | 0.17 | 1.7 | 0.29 |
| Brand Damage | 0 | 1.7 | 0.00 |
| Stalling new innovation | 0.12 | 1.3 | 0.16 |
| Threat to sustain industries | 0 | 2.7 | 0.00 |
| **TOTAL** | 1 | | 1.69 |

## SWOT Map

The SWOT Map enables you to demonstrate direct alignment of the strategies and goals of the team to the strengths, weaknesses, opportunities and threats that you have just analyzed. Note: There is absolutely no math involved in this activity. All you need is a little time, a small dose of common sense, and a BOLD mindset to quickly map these foundational elements together. While we understand common sense really isn't that common and time is not something we have an abundance of, we're confident that if you approach this activity BOLD-ly, you will successfully provide this powerful map to your teams with little or no pain to yourself.

The first step is to number and list each of the strengths, weaknesses, opportunities and threats in their respective areas on the table below. The next step is to review each of the strategies and goals and see if (and where) they are supported by the strengths, challenged by the weaknesses, and are helping pursue opportunities to defend against threats. Accordingly, place each of the strategies and goals in one of the four quadrants on the table below, and note which strategies or goals do not fit in any of the quadrants.

The correct placement is identified by reviewing and recognizing where each of these actions align to the strengths, weaknesses, opportunities and threats. For example, where you have a strategy that aligns with your strengths and is also focused on defending one or more of your threats, you place that item in the quadrant for Strength to Threat (S-T).

Finally, list the specific strength, weakness, opportunity or threat in parenthesis behind the actions in each quadrant. In the previous S-T example, if the action aligns with strengths 1 and 2 from your list and threat 3, you would record this as (S1, S2, T3). The completed map enables you to either demonstrate the validity of the team's actions or identify where they may be on the wrong path. The following is an example of a completed SWOT Map.

| | Strengths | Weakness |
|---|---|---|
| | 1. Technical Knowledge<br>2. Organizational Knowledge<br>3. Structured Process<br>4. Aware of Blind Spot<br>5. Committed to Organization<br>6. Business Acumen | 1. Little Flexibility<br>2. Fear (Displacement, change, new workplace)<br>3. Technology Deficiencies<br>4. Lack of Trust<br>5. Exasperation<br>6. Don't acknowledge/recognize value millennials |
| **Opportunities** | **S-O Strategies** | **W-O Strategies** |
| 1. Learning from millennial<br>2. Form mutually beneficial partnerships<br>3. Increase the ability to attract millennials<br>4. Educate midlevel managers to share knowledge and experience<br>5. Redefine relevant retention targets for millennials | 1. Set up partnerships to learn from one another; across generations (S1, S2, S3, S5, O2, O4)<br>2. Social events with mid-managers and Millennials (S3, S5, O1, O2) | 1. Mini town-halls within departments. Getting more feedback from the analyst level (W2, W4, W5, W6, O1, O4)<br>2. Managers will have frequent focus group session with direct reports to get feedback & suggestions (W2, W4, W5, W6, O1, O4) |
| **Threats** | **S-T Strategies** | **W-T Strategies** |
| 1. High turnover (cost)<br>2. Brand Damage<br>3. Stalling new innovation<br>4. Threat to sustain industries | 1. Create a leadership development program for Millennials with action learning projects sponsored by Mid-Managers (S1, S2, S5, S6, T1) | 1. Training/education for managers (W1, W2, W3, T1, T3) |

*Culture Pulse*

The purpose of the Culture Pulse is to rapidly gauge the underlying thoughts and feelings of a team or organization. Thoughts and feelings are the foundational elements of culture and a significant predictor of the success and sustainability of strategy. Strategic success is dramatically increased when positive and inclusive thoughts and feelings are shared amongst the team. Strategies have little to no chance of success when the thoughts and feelings are predominantly negative and divisive. So why is this indicator of success often overlooked?

**Unlike Tim's 6ᵗʰ grade teacher, Sister Mary JoAnn, we can't read minds.**

We are often unaware of the collective thoughts and feelings of our teams because, unlike Tim's 6ᵗʰ grade teacher, Sister Mary JoAnn, we can't read minds. We rely on what we can see in results and behaviors and take the nodding heads of passive agreement to represent a rousing chorus of "hell yeah and let's get to work!" In reality, *Complacent Bunnies* may be up to their old tricks, and the nodding heads are simply a way our team is greeting their old friend. This is where leveraging the Culture Pulse will momentarily give you the ability to consider the thoughts and feelings of your team, identify previously hidden catalysts and barriers to success, and drive a sense of ownership and empowerment to the team.

The Culture Pulse is simply a list of archetypical words that represent positivity and inclusion on one extreme and negativity and division on the other. The list we use has forty thoughts and feelings included. The task of the team is to simply identify as many of the words as possible that describe how they are thinking and feeling in that moment, as it relates to their team. They must identify at least one word (as everyone has at least one feeling), and they can identify with as many of the words as they want. The Culture Pulse can be presented to the team on a piece of paper, through a polling tool, through email or even on a bar napkin if the setting is right. The key is to keep it simple and anonymous for the team. This concept was first introduced to us by Art & Carol Paton. After working with multiple teams globally, the following is the list we currently use:

| | | | |
|---|---|---|---|
| Afraid | Doubtful | Interested | Scared |
| Against It | Energized | Irate | Settled |
| Angry | Excited | Isolated | Shy |
| Anxious | Excluded | Nervous | Skeptical |
| Capable | Friendly | Proactive | Supportive |
| Challenged | Happy | Ready | Uncertain |
| Comfortable | Helpful | Relieved | Uninterested |
| Confident | Hopeful | Respected | Unprepared |
| Confused | Included | Reactive | Upset |
| Disrespected | Informed | Sad | Valued |

No matter how the Culture Pulse is presented, you simply need to collect the responses from each team member and perform a quick analysis of the data. The analysis includes the following:

- Tally each time one of the words is identified.
- Determine the response percentage for each word by dividing the total tallies from each word by the total number of participants and multiplying it by 100%.
- Identify the words with large percentages of responses and determine whether these are positive and inclusive thoughts and feelings, or those of negativity and division.
- Summarize the story that this data has provided.

Once the analysis is complete, share the data and the story with the team. We often present the data as a bar graph with a summary of the story on a single slide as shown below. If the data reflects the desired thoughts and feelings of positivity and inclusion, take a moment to celebrate. Where it shows a more negative or divisive undertone, pause, recognize the potential issue and seek out a leader to address the culture gaps you just surfaced. The following is an example of the Culture Pulse Summary:

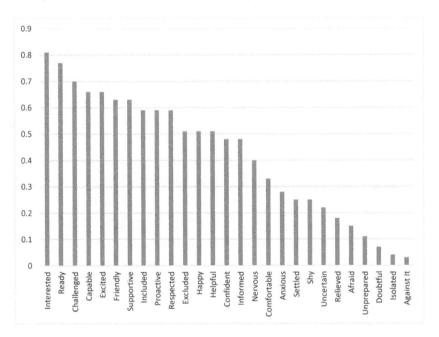

The culture pulse highlights the interest, readiness, confidence and excitement of the team. It also indicated the team's positive sense of being included and respected.

## Reader Practice:

*Practice 1- Start with yourself*

Identify your personal strengths, weaknesses, opportunities and threats for a specific project you are working on and list the current strategies or goals you have for this project. Complete the IFE, EFE, SWOT Map with your input only.

- What did your IFE score tell you about your personal strengths and weaknesses?
- What key strengths should you be leveraging for this project?
- What weaknesses need to be addressed immediately to increase your ability to be successful?
- What did your EFE score tell you about the opportunities and threats for this project?
- What opportunities or threats should you prioritize?
- What does the SWOT Map tell you about the alignment of your strategies and goals to your strengths, weaknesses, opportunities and threats?
- What actions should you take now that you have this information?

Assemble a group of trusted colleagues, friends or family members to practice with the Modified SWOT tools and the Culture Pulse. Complete the IFE, EFE, SWOT Map and Culture Pulse for a shared project or social outing. Make sure your topic is relevant and shared with the group of "cool kids" you are practicing with, and that you get experience in collecting and analyzing the group's input. Upon completion of the session, make sure to get their feedback. Ask them the following questions and be open and grateful for their input:

- What did I do well in this session?
- What step in the process do I need to improve on most?
- What was I most comfortable with?
- What will I do differently next time?

Complete the Culture Pulse for yourself. Don't worry about calculating percentages, just focus on the thoughts and feelings you selected.

- What does the information tell you about the probability of success for this project?
- What actions should you take to enhance your feeling of positivity and inclusion?
- How would you share the story you developed with the modified SWOT tools and the Culture Pulse with your friends (real or imaginary), spouse, children, boss, project sponsor or client?
- What response would you like to experience when you share your story?

*Practice 2- Try it with a team*

Practice the same exercise described earlier with a team.

## CHAPTER RECAP

- This chapter focused on capturing the feelings that will drive or hinder your efforts. The Culture Pulse will momentarily give you the ability to consider the thoughts and feelings of your team, identify previously hidden catalysts and barriers to success, and drive a sense of ownership and empowerment to the team.
- We discussed the importance of aligning strategies and goals with the realities of your current strengths, weaknesses, opportunities and threats, as well as the underlying thoughts and feelings embedded within the culture. This alignment is critical to increase the probability of achieving the ideal outcomes you envision, and to ensure your strategies and goals are truly leading you toward the results you desire.
- Using our Modified SWOT analysis provides you with quantitative data to measure alignment, and a simple map to identify this alignment and potential gaps.

- The combination of these tools enables you to identify and mitigate the two key tricks of the *Complacent Bunny*.
  ○ The first trick is a magic powder that blinds us from truly understanding the realities of our organizations, teams, and the external environment within which they operate.
  ○ The second trick forces us to ignore the underlying thoughts and feelings of our organizations, concerning our strategies.
- Successfully leveraging these tools requires you to be BOLD, set aside any fears you have about a little math, and be willing to ask about and address the worst F-word in group settings---Feelings.

In this chapter, you have learned how to identify and address the tricks of the *Complacent Bunnies*. Unfortunately, some of their cousins are still lurking. The next chapter will provide insight and tools to avoid the traps set by the *Culture Rabbit*.

# CHAPTER 7
## BUILDING BEHAVIOR BRIDGES

*"Culture eats strategy for breakfast."*
**– Peter Drucker**

**In the previous** chapter, we discussed how the Modified SWOT and Culture Pulse can mitigate the tricks of the *Complacent Bunny*. This chapter will focus on how BOLD people and teams achieve predictable success by building behavior bridges (linking behaviors to results). When *Culture Rabbits* get the scent of BOLD leaders who are serious about changing behaviors to achieve results, they get *hopping mad* and leave the garden for other pastures!

These BOLD people appear to transform culture with ease by focusing on high standards of excellence. They begin with the end in mind and connect the dots with predictive indicators to gain momentum. The other skill BOLD people apply to send the *Culture Rabbit* packing is being open to learn from their failures.

> There are *huge* benefits for leaders who can predict the success or failure of important initiatives early.

There are *huge* benefits for leaders who can predict the success or failure of important initiatives early. This is worth repeating...There are *huge* benefits for those who can predict the success or failure of important initiatives early. Impact Mapping is an efficient process to help you do this.

The leading authority on Impact Maps is Robert O. Brinkerhoff, who established the link between competency and key behaviors

69

leading to predictable results. Creating an Impact Map can be a simple, yet powerful tool, to measure early success or failure.

*Reader Reflection*

- *What predictive measures do you use to gauge the success or failure of your initiative?*
- *What questions should you start asking to gauge an initiative's success or failure?*
- *What are the early indicators that provide evidence you are winning over the Culture Rabbit?*
- *When did you last "kill" a project early? What were the reasons?*

*Tools/Principles of the Chapter*

If you're the solutions architect (the person tasked with designing and implementing solutions), using an Impact Map early in your strategy allows you to see the clear line of sight between knowledge/skills, behaviors, results and outcomes/goals.

Impact Maps come in many shapes and sizes. Some maps may have over a dozen columns. Our moto follows the "keep it simple" principle, so our preference is using a four-column map. This allows us to create an Impact Map in one hour or less.

We were asked to create an organizational strategy for managers to attract and retain millennials. The map identified the following line of sight to the goal (identified from the magic wand exercise in chapter three). We then identified leading results for attaining the goal. The next step was to capture the key behaviors, along with the supporting knowledge and skills for their role.

Please see the following example of a completed Impact Map:

| Knowledge and Skills | Key Behaviors | Key Results | Desired State |
|---|---|---|---|
| • Blended listening skills<br>• Coaching / Reverse-Mentoring<br>• Risk management<br>• Learn technology (i.e. social media)<br>• Increase knowledge of work policies<br>• Constructive feedback skills | 1. Proactive Feedback and communication<br>2. Flexibility (where, when and how)<br>3.Encourage creativity and innovation<br>4. Challenge millennials with stretch assignments<br>5. Seek to actively learn from millennials | A. Reduced millennial turnover<br>B. Increased millennial referrals<br>C. Increased millennial retention<br>D. Increased and improved development opportunities and outcomes<br>E. Increased 'Glass Door' recommendations | Our mid-level managers will cultivate an innovative and balanced workplace where they provide fre-quent feedback and coaching, project-based learning and drive engage-ment.<br><br>They will demonstrate respect for the value each millennial brings to the organization by proactively learning about new technolo-gies, engag-ing in reverse mentoring |

## Create an Impact Map

The ingredients you will need:

- ✓ A computer with an electronic version of the Impact Map is optional; a flip chart and markers will do just as well.
- ✓ A conference room with participants (3-10) who know most about the initiative or goal.
- ✓ A best practice we recommend is having one person facili-tating the discussion and another person recording the in-formation into the Impact Map template.

Identify the target audience that is critical to achieve the goal; this could be supervisors, managers, customer support specialists etc. In many cases, you may need to complete an Impact Map for multiple target audiences. If you are unfamiliar with the target audience, do some homework. Meet with team members, observe their work, and ask to view their job description. Your session outcomes will be more robust and successful when you know more about the roles.

When scheduling the Impact Map session, select individuals who clearly understand the goal of the initiative. Before the session begins, add the name of the target audience at the top of the page of your Impact Map template. Then enter the goal statement (if it is already completed from the magic wand exercise in chapter 3) into the far-right column of the template. If the goal is still undefined, have the discussion first to clarify the goal or desired state with participants. This is key, as you want to start with the end in mind.

Introduce the Impact Map, review the target audience and the desired goal. Then ask participants to identify and list key individual or team results which provide evidence that the goal has been achieved or not. We like to spend the time and effort necessary to uncover *leading* versus *lagging* indicators. A leading indicator can help predict significant future changes, while a lagging indicator confirms that a pattern is occurring.

After capturing results, we then ask the group to identify and list key behaviors they believe would contribute to the results. Key behaviors are those that will tip the scale by supporting multiple results.

After you have the list of behaviors recorded, brainstorm a list of knowledge or skills that enable and support the key behaviors for the target audience.

Once the Impact Map is drafted, we validate the Impact Map using story-telling. We accomplish this by asking them to share a story that describes what knowledge and skills are essential to support key behaviors. Then we ask them to describe which behaviors have the most impact on results. Lastly, they share what results are essential to indicate their goal is achieved. We isolate the critical behaviors that impact the most results, enabling us to achieve the desired goal.

After the Impact Map is validated, your solution and evaluation process now becomes clear. If your initiative requires creating learning programs to support the goal, the amount of content required and the time necessary for developing learning content is significantly shorter. As a best practice, we like to include the Impact Map in the training material for the target audience. This allows them to see the big picture of how applying the critical behaviors will deliver the results and desired state.

*Ready – Fire – Aim?*

We were asked to evaluate a learning program focused on improving communication. Our objective was to help the target audience (including individual contributors and supervisors) to proactively escalate issues for decision-making. The initiative included an emphasis on training. They had the metrics on the number of "butts-in-seats," in addition to  participant feedback regarding the training experience they received. Attendee feedback on the training sessions was favorable. We gave kudos to the leadership team for adding change agents, who played an integral role in assisting with the launch. They were then able to sustain the momentum throughout the program's lifecycle.

We met with the integration team to complete an Impact Map. The result provided us a clear line of sight – linking learning, behaviors, results and goals for the initiative. We received a list of participants who attended the program so we could solicit their feedback in an effort to learn about their experiences.

We developed a short survey which was sent to the target audience, who recently completed the training. The survey included a question to determine if they achieved any results using the key behavior taught in the program. The response to the question included four possible answers:

- *I applied the behavior with positive results.*
- *I applied the behavior but not sure of the results.*
- *I was already applying the behavior before the training.*
- *I will not be applying the behavior.*

The survey results revealed a big surprise. An overwhelming response indicated they were already applying the behaviors before the training program. So, you may be asking yourself at this point, *"What was causing the issue if the individual contributors and supervisors had already been applying the behavior before the training?"* The bottleneck was further upstream -- above the supervisor level. The results allowed leadership to take appropriate action necessary to remove the bottleneck and achieve success.

## CHAPTER RECAP

- Impact Maps help take the guesswork out of culture work by isolating the few critical behaviors that will deliver results and support the goals for your initiative.
- Impact Maps come in all shapes and sizes. It depends on the information you are trying to obtain and use.
- Consider measuring the impact behaviors have on your next improvement initiative. Don't wait too long to make your decision, as the *Culture Rabbits* may have already eaten your Cheerios!

This chapter focused on creating an Impact Map, establishing the line of sight from knowledge and skills, while enabling critical behaviors that unleash desired results and outcomes.

Using Impact Maps can start a counter-culture revolution; moving your enterprise from *being stuck* - to one that is *game on*. The next chapter is critical to support energetic leaders from falling off the ledge.

**Impact Maps can start a counter-culture revolution; moving your enterprise from *being stuck* - to one that is *game on*.**

# CHAPTER 8
# LEDGE WALKING

*"I'm very accident-prone. The problem is
I sort of just do things. I'm impulsive,
and sometimes I don't think."*

**~ Tom Cullen**

**Many times, in** our professional and personal lives, we feel like we are walking on a very narrow ledge between success and failure. One small misstep or hesitation may cause us to fall off the cliff and fail. If we do not have the courage to take a step, or are too hasty in our decision, we may not reach the destination we desire. These moments are even more frequent when we are leading a team. We are not only responsible for our own personal success and safety, but we carry the responsibility for the people who have entrusted us to help them navigate these treacherous ledges. Just to make things more challenging, we often encounter the very loud and proud *Ledge-Walking Rabbits* at these critical moments.

These pesky little friends have a heart of gold and truly want us (and our teams) to succeed. They may encourage us to look straight ahead and act without fear of our surroundings, or they may also advise of the dangers ahead before taking one more step. In the moment, they help leaders believe their action (or inaction) is truly the right decision. Our primary responsibility is to capture the *Ledge-Walking Rabbit* so we can help these leaders quickly align their immediate thoughts to their environment, and be ready to quickly release these action-driven friends at the right moment (to pull leaders from the ledge of failure, or push them off the ledge of success).

In this chapter, we familiarize you with three key tools to help you BOLD-ly capture and leverage the *Ledge-Walking Rabbit*. Our adaption of the Issue Description Tool from Susan Scott's book *Fierce Conversations* is a quick and simple way of helping leaders understand the challenges they are facing and clearly communicate the help needed from the team in that moment. The Ledge-Walking tool provides you with an easy process to help leaders see both the risks and rewards of simply relying on training alone for their teams to achieve success.

We will then unleash the power of a "Bar Napkin" to playfully map the Ledge-Walking experience. Finally, we will share an innovative method that combines the tools we have covered to create a robust strategy in Four-Hours! Using this process enables you to capture the *Ledge-Walking Rabbit*, while ensuring his cousins and PER friends are kept in check as you help leaders navigate the ledges of success and failure.

*I'll Take that Bet*

We were working with a leadership team to implement a massive reorganization. Senior leadership was aggressively breaking down functional silos and mandating increased collaboration. The direction was clear -- make it happen! These leaders were quickly frustrated with the perceived lack of urgency and the inability of their teams to tangibly identify, resolve and show benefits of this glorious and mandated dream state. While we were meeting to discuss how to help the team move forward, the *Ledge-Walking Rabbit* took its seat at the head of the table and aggressively pushed these leaders toward the edge of a hasty course of action, centered on re-training their teams.

We interjected, and challenged them to think of ways to mitigate the issues they were experiencing; but that darn rabbit stood loud and proud and kept the team on a collision course with failure. In that moment, we Bold-ly leveraged the competitive nature of the group and the provocative voice of the *Ledge-Walking Rabbit* to help pull them from the ledge -- in the most authentic and playful way we could. We bet them: if given less than an hour to explain the exact details of what success looked like, and four hours with the team that was frustrating them, we could gain strategic alignment and accelerate the results they required.

**If we succeeded, they would get the credit; if we failed, they had the luxury of blaming us.**

We even upped the ante by wagering a case of beer, and included our tried-and-true guarantee. They promised us a case of beer (good Belgian beer, not the crappy stuff) if we could make this happen within the time frame, and we would do so in kind if we failed. In addition (as our tried-and-true guarantee states), if we succeeded, they would get the credit; if we failed, they had the luxury of blaming us. The leaders and the *Ledge-Walking Rabbit* quickly took the bet.

With the remaining fifteen minutes of that meeting, we took the opportunity to have them articulate more about the issues they were facing, by using the Issue Description Tool. Each of the leaders were given three minutes and twenty-two seconds (the length of one of our favorite songs – "Sweet Caroline") to individually complete the tool. We played the song for them as a form of inspiration and urgency. They feverishly worked to complete the tool (in the competitive nature they did all things) and were ready to discuss their input right on time. We spent the next ten minutes discussing and aligning the details each had provided, and then scheduled a meeting with them for the remainder of the forty-five minutes they had promised us.

At the beginning of the next session, we reviewed the consolidated Issue Description Tool, made some minor edits, and then gave them each a bar napkin. *If your Legal and HR departments have an objection to a bar napkin in the workplace, then use a picnic napkin. (It's the same napkin, choose your battles wisely.)

We walked the team through the Ledge-Walking process and they recorded their responses for each section on their napkin. At the end of this meeting (which started late due to their late arrival--but *still* finished right on time), we had everything needed for our Four-Hour Strategy session.

The Four-Hour session was a fast-paced and collaborative experience. We shared the output of meetings with their leaders and the team eased into exploring the official and ground truth of the situation. Many PERs were trying to find a way to influence (and sometimes even derail) the process, but we had planned for them to make an appearance, and used many of the performance tools described in previous chapters to catch them. In less than four hours, we had delivered on our commitment to gain alignment and move the team to action.

The funny thing is, we still lost the bet. The leaders (and their *Ledge-Walking Rabbit* friend) pointed out that our wager did not include the thirty minute debrief with them after the Four-Hour session, and thus took more time than we had stated. We gladly provided the case of Belgian Beer wagered; it was a small price to pay to keep the *Ledge-Walking Rabbit* in check, and to eliminate organizational pain and suffering that was soon to occur if we did not Bold-ly get these leaders to "take the bet!"

*Reader Reflection*

---

- *Recall a project where the Ledge-Walking Rabbit was pushing your leaders or teams toward failure.*
  - ○ *What was the Rabbit saying or doing?*
  - ○ *What decisions or actions were going to lead to more issues or failure?*
  - ○ *What was the impact to your project, team or organization?*
- *Describe the issue the team was facing in two sentences or less.*
  - ○ *Were you able to effectively describe the issue?*
  - ○ *How would this have benefited your team?*
  - ○ *How can you Bold-ly leverage the competitive nature of leaders to move them away from the dangers of the Ledge-Walking Rabbit?*

*Tools/Principles of the Chapter*

---

*Issue Description Tool*

As previously mentioned, the Issue Description is our adaptation of the tool from Susan Scott's book *Fierce Conversations*. Susan does a great job of providing a simple tool to define the issue you are working on, and to describe the importance of the issue. She then explains the vital step of clearly and humbly requesting the assistance you are seeking. The only subtle (yet impactful) change we've made to her process is to add an additional emphasis on the urgency of the issue we are working on. Too many times, we blur the lines of significance and urgency. The sheer fact that we need something *now* does not make it significant. The following is the template we use.

| Criteria | Issue Definition |
|---|---|
| THE ISSUE IS: | |
| IT IS SIGNIFICANT BECAUSE: | |
| THE URGENCY OF THIS ISSUE IS: | |
| MY IDEAL OUTCOME IS: | |
| RELEVANT BACKGROUND INFORMATION: | |
| WHAT I HAVE DONE UP TO THIS POINT: | |
| THE HELP I WANT FROM YOU IS: | |

The first step in using the Issue Description Tool is to define the issue at hand. The issue should be able to be stated in two sentences or less. If this can't be accomplished, then you have a different issue. This tells you the issue is either not known or it cannot be presented in a simple or clear enough manner for a team to understand and take action. Once the issue is clearly stated, then move on to identify the significance and urgency of the issue.

The significance of the issue should be rooted in one of the following: what good things will happen once the issue is resolved, or what bad things will pay us a visit if it is not resolved. The urgency occurs when significant things could go wrong if the issue is not resolved. This is one of the slippery slopes upon which the PERs are waiting to greet us. They are constantly pushing every issue as a "must-do-now" scenario. Capturing them at this juncture enables us to accurately prioritize the issues we are facing and gives one of the best gifts in the world.... TIME. Each of the issues we are working on have significance or we wouldn't be addressing them, but they all don't have the same urgency. Every month, day, hour or minute counts, so being able to state the urgency of the issue is absolutely critical.

Next, be BOLD and state the ideal outcome you are looking for when the issue is resolved. This step takes both courage and humility, and requires you to be able to understand and clearly state the result you are seeking. This step provides the bookends to the story of the issue you are resolving, and also gives insight to the team of where you expect them to be at the end of the issue-resolving journey. Being able to see the finish line is a powerful way to keep the team from falling prey to the *Ledge-Walking Rabbit*.

**Being able to state the urgency of the issue is absolutely critical.**

Now, provide relevant background information to the issue and set context for what has been done to date. Be BOLD, but simple, in this step. This is not an opportunity to work on your dissertation writing skills or for you to brag about all the work you've done. Use a handful of bullet points in each section of the template to help the team gain a deeper understanding and appreciation of the issue being addressed. Finally, request help from the tea

The request for help must be realistic and time bound. A request for help without a due date is just a wish. Make sure to gain agreement and commitment on the request you are making, and be open to negotiating both timing and the way the help is given— provided it aligns with both the issue you are working to resolve, and the related urgency.

The total time to complete this template is only the length of your favorite song. We use this tool to prepare issues we are working on, as well as having the teams we work with define the issues they are facing. Once completed, you and your teams can practice presenting the issues to critical stakeholders prior to having the real conversations. You can work through the tool and rehearse presenting it in less than fifteen minutes.

**A request for help without a due date is just a wish.**

*Reader Practice*

- Complete the Issue Description Tool for an issue you are currently facing at work, home or within your community.
  - ○ What did you learn from defining the significance and urgency of the issue?
  - ○ What challenges do you expect to get from the ideal outcomes or help you are requesting?
  - ○ Who will you present this issue to?
- Practice with a friend or group: Have your friend or group complete the Issue Description Tool for an issue they are facing. Ask them the following:
  - ○ What was their overall experience with the tool?
  - ○ What was the hardest part for them?
  - ○ What challenges do they expect to encounter when they share this issue with their intended audience?

*Ledge Walking Technology (Bar Napkin Activity)*

Ledge Walking Technology (LWT) is a creative blend of performance technology tools to support the action-driven needs of our leaders. The innovative nature of this conceptual blend breathes new life into the tried and true standard tools of performance technology, and leverages colorful story-telling techniques to playfully keep our teams and leaders engaged. The practical application of LWT enables the performance technologist to rapidly identify, select and communicate both instructional and non-instructional solutions that drive the desired results our leaders envision (without causing numb butts and bloodshot eyes from excessive and ineffective training or meetings). Each of these systematic stages of the performance technology process presents us with challenges we like to call *ledges*. It is on these ledges that the ever-present and influential Ledge-Walking Rabbit waits to meet us.

The ability to identify the need for instructional, non-instructional, or blended solutions is the first ledge that we have encountered. Leaders often come to us with the predetermined answer to their problem. The conversation starts off with: *"We need you to build training for us, probably e-learning. We don't have a budget for this, but we know you can meet this need. Oh, and we need it next week."*

We know you were either laughing or crying as you read this, and if you are like us, you'd love to push this leader off whatever ledge you could find! It is in moments like this, however, when we need to fight the urge to push them off the ledge. The next best option is to begin a minimal needs analysis to salvage any benefits from the time and effort already invested. The best solution is to BOLD-ly walk with these leaders for a short time on this ledge, and enlighten them with grace, patience and resolve.

Getting leaders to relate the impact of their desired state (in terms of the organization) is one of the more difficult ledges to navigate. This is the ledge where a dream meets reality, and can generate the Mt. Everest of resistance and fear of failure. We help leaders make the organizational connection between the impact of their desired state and the potentially hasty action they are requiring. We help them articulate the impact their actions will have on the results they are seeking for their organization. They may be wanting to increase productivity, decrease waste, improve retention of top talent or impact customer satisfaction scores. The process should be completed within 5-10 minutes and is heavily dependent on your ability to BOLD-ly capture the Ledge-Walking Rabbit and help put the entire system in view for the leader. We accomplish this by arming the leader with a bar napkin.

The bar napkin activity provides the leader a fun and quick way to establish a deeper understanding of the organizational metrics they are truly seeking. Start by handing out a bar napkin to participants and asking them to unfold the napkin so they can see all four squares or quadrants. Next, have them label each quadrant with the following titles as shown in the image below:

- Initiatives
- Solutions
- Tax, Staff Benefit or Business Driver
- Key Behaviors

**The bar napkin activity provides the leader a fun and quick way to establish a deeper understanding of the organizational metrics**

Initiatives

1. Leader Dev.
2. Optimize process
3. Reduce sales cycle
4. Annual Expense
   Reporting Training

Tax, Staff Benefit or Business Driver

1. Staff benefit
2. Bus. Driver
3. Bus. Driver
4. Tax

Solutions

1. I (Instruction)
2. NI (Non-Instructional)
3. BL (Blended)
4. I (Instruction)

Key behaviors

1. Pro-active
2. Simplify the complex
3. Client partner
4. Ethics and Compliant

©Performance Journey Partners, LLC

Now the real fun begins.

Ask the group to write down the top three initiatives they are focusing on in the top left quadrant. Make sure they know they do not need to provide details of the initiative; they simply need to be able to name it at this point. For each of the initiatives, ask the group to list the solutions they feel will drive the results they require in the bottom left quadrant. Then for each solution they propose, have the participants place an I, NI or B next to the individual solution to identify it as follows:

I = Instructional solution (communication, training, assessment)

NI = Non-instructional solution (software change, process simplification, coaching)

BL = Blended (combination on instructional and non-instructional solutions)

The purpose of this is to see if the *One-Hit Wabbit* has joined the party, and if the group or leader you are working with is approaching their needs from a more systems-oriented view.

In our world, a tax is an instructional solution where the primary purpose of the training is measured by the number of people who complete it. It is a quick way to check a box and be able to provide documented evidence of its completion. This approach is a common attempt to meet the increased regulatory requirements of many of our industries. A staff benefit is an instructional solution where the primary purpose of the training is to ensure that the participants enjoyed the session and may have learned something new. This approach is often used as a part of retention efforts for organizational talent. A business driver is an instructional solution that has a direct link to one of the defined organizational goals. This approach is used to align human capital to the real needs of the business. It can be measured in realized business terms such as: increased productivity, reduction in re-work, and increased proficiency in critical on the job behaviors.

We have found that most people we work with conclude that many of their recommended solutions are either blended or fall victim to being a tax on the organization. Therefore, we then ask them to capture the behaviors they expect to be impacted by the solutions. We remind them that these can be changes in existing behaviors, behaviors that are new, or those that simply need to stop. This data set directly links back to the impact map described earlier in this book, and helps establish a much better line of sight regarding how these enhanced behaviors will drive business results. You will also see what key knowledge and skills are foundational to ensuring a successful result from the proposed solution. The total output from the bar napkin can be used to quickly align solutions, keep the *One-Hit-Wonder Wabbit* at bay, and generate a very succinct elevator speech for leaders.

Give it a try! Grab a bar napkin and follow the steps above for the issues you are working on at home, at work or within your community. The total activity should only take 10 minutes.

- *What PERs were sitting on your shoulder during the activity?*
- *What were they saying?*
- *How did you silence them as you completed the activity?*
- *Where are you going to try to use this tool "for real?"*

### Create a Robust Strategy in Four Hours

The Four-Hour Strategy is a creative sequencing of many of the tools described throughout this book. The ideal outcome is to be able to quickly and collaboratively lead a group to a strategy in less than four hours. Delivering on this promise requires you to be extremely BOLD and we strongly encourage using co-facilitators to maintain your sanity and blood pressure during this very high-energy session. The following is the process we follow.

| Tool | Outcome | ~Time (Mins) |
|------|---------|--------------|
| **Official vs. Ground Truth** | Interrogate Reality | 15 |
| **Magic Wand/Desired State** | Focus on Results | 20 |
| **Rapid Gap Analysis (RGA)** | Categorize Causal Factors | 45 |
| **Modified SWOT** | Guide Leader Actions | 60 |
| **21 Activity – Speed Dating for Results** | Target Solutions | 30 |
| **Culture Pulse** | Assess Change Readiness | 10 |
| **Impact Map** | Build Behavioral Bridge | 40 |
| **Executive Summary** | Summarize Strategy | 20 |

©Performance Journey Partners, LLC

All the tools listed, except the strategy summary, have detailed instructions in previous chapters. We recommend some additional things to consider when facilitating this session. First of all, make sure that you and your co-facilitator are aligned with the tools you will be presenting. Secondly, the expectation is that you will have collected, collated and presented the output from the session before closing it. This will keep you both hopping the entire session. Lastly, it is critical to keep a close eye on the dynamics of the groups you are working with to ensure those darn PERs aren't showing up and derailing the process.

Open the session with brief introductions and then immediately jump into the Official vs Ground Truth activity. This is key to trust-building, and foundational to setting the tone for the day. Once the debrief for this section is completed, immediately move into defining a desired state. Once the feedback has been collected, one of the facilitators will conduct the analysis and generate the desired state, while the other moves the team into the Rapid Gap Analysis. The desired state needs to be shared with the group prior to the debrief of the Rapid Gap Analysis. Additionally, one of the facilitators needs to be transcribing the data from the analysis to ensure you are prepared for the debrief prior to closing the section. Before taking a break, collect the list of strengths, weaknesses, opportunities and threats.

Once participants return from their break, collect the remainder of the information needed to complete the Modified SWOT analysis. This is one of the more draining activities on the group--so watch out for *the Ledge-Walking* and *Complacent Rabbits*. They love to show up during this section of the session and wreak havoc on many of the team members. Once you push through the Modified SWOT, the group is re-energized from the 21 Activity. As one facilitator conducts the Culture Pulse and Impact Map, the other should be recording the results of the 21 Activity, preparing the effort/benefit matrix and drafting the Executive Summary for the end of the session. The Executive Summary is simply a bulleted slide that provides the key outputs and messages from the strategy session and provides a brief synopsis of next steps.

*Reader Practice*

- Practice with a group or family members: Have your group complete the Four Hour strategy process for a sports team or movie/TV cast. Keep it light and fun. Once you have completed the process reflect on the following:

○ What went well?

○ What do I need to work on to be ready for the real deal?

○ What are some teams I should approach to leverage this process?

## CHAPTER RECAP

- This chapter focused on tools that target and identify situations where we need to pull leaders and teams from the many ledges of failure, and when we need to push them off the ledge so they can achieve the success they envision.

- The issue description tool enables us to clearly identify the issue we are addressing, presenting the ideal outcomes of resolving these issues, and asking for assistance with courage and humility.

- The bar napkin provides us with a fun and simple way to capture the *One-Hit-Wonder Wabbit* and align our leaders and teams with the behaviors we are trying to enhance or eliminate.

- The Four-Hour Strategy process takes what is traditionally a painful, time-consuming and labor intensive effort, and allows us to develop a robust strategy in four hours or less.

In this chapter, you have learned how to navigate the many ledges of success and failures you experience. The next chapter will provide insight and methods to take what you've learned in this book and pay it forward for yourself and others.

# CHAPTER 9
## Paying it forward

*"What we do for ourselves dies with us. What we do for others and the world remains and is immortal."*

**~ Albert Pine**

**Leveraging the** "Law of Abundance" is essential for leaders and practitioners to break the self-centered paradigm of knowledge being power, and avoid falling into the variability of the vast amount of information that social media provides. Leaders and organizations who do this well pay it forward by sharing skills, insights, expertise and, yes, even failures with others to enhance continual improvement of workers, the organization, and the global society.

You have probably heard the saying: "A good leader knows the way – shows the way – then goes away," leaving a sustainable enterprise for the next wave of success. To *lead the way* demands paying it forward, by sharing lessons learned from their day-to-day experiences with their team and others.

BOLD people who do this well shamelessly share their skills, expertise and failures to help others make a more significant impact. Through this exchange, we may think only the receiver is the beneficiary.

> **BOLD people who do this well shamelessly share their skills, expertise and failures to help others make a more significant impact.**

However, we believe that the benefit is three-fold:

- the giver
- the receiver
- the people who are recipients of both.

We are very intentional about looking for ways to initiate this pay it forward mentality.

*Reader Reflection:*

- *What was your moment when someone came alongside you and ignited your passion?*
- *What were their names and what role did they play?*
- *What did they do that may have altered your purpose?*
- *Who else came along by your side and supported you?*
- *Who are you actively sharing your expertise with?*

Here are some simple yet profound ways you can personally and professionally begin the pay it forward experience.

*Day in the Life*

One way we pay it forward is to offer what is called a *"Day in the Life"* event in which people both inside and outside our organization, from various backgrounds and expertise, come to spend a day with us to share innovative ideas, insight and tools. It is a fast-paced, intense experience that provides participants the opportunity to share, grow, and apply new ways of systems thinking and performance improvement in their respective roles.

We compare it to a group of doctors who conduct morning rounds in a university teaching hospital. They immerse themselves collectively to contribute expertise and recommendations that benefit the outcomes for each patient.

Our *"Day in the Life"* focuses on the work we do as performance consultants, as well as our actual day-to-day experiences -- which include catching PERs. Colleagues from diverse backgrounds are offered the opportunity to experience the success, failures and challenges. We then practice using performance improvement tools in real scenarios that participants bring with them.

To make it more interesting, the agenda is totally blank slate, with no set format. We focus on what participants want to walk away with at the end of the day. The blank slate agenda allows participants to spend segments of time with different team members on various topics.

The end of the day incorporates a roundtable discussion with everyone sharing their observations and insight. We commonly experience seeing everyone's knowledge and skills sharpened and relationships deepened. We often learn more from our guests than what we have shared with them. The cost of the event to the participants is only an $8 lunch ticket; the outcome is priceless!

*Playing Up*

A common practice with sports teams is to have junior athletes play with (or against) more advanced players. Coaches typically do this to enhance the skill level of both the junior player and their team. The goal is to boost their skills, and take their game up a notch. The junior team members participate with those who are more experienced and have greater skill and intuition. Smart coaches are looking at the bigger picture. They are not just interested in the score, but more importantly, they are interested in what the athlete learned (and if their skills have improved). If the advanced players are also mentoring (sharing knowledge and game experience) with the junior team, the advanced players further develop their mentoring skills. BOLD managers look for opportunities for their team members to *play up* to sharpen their organizational skills.

*Active Mentoring & Coaching*
*Kery's story*

In sixth grade, I started playing the drums in band. I remember the day my band director took me from study hall into the main band room with two sparkling drum kits and the senior drummer from jazz band. We each sat down on a drum set. He asked me to start playing along with him, working on various rhythms. That one simple mentoring event transformed my practice routines (and more importantly), my passion and drive for playing drums that is still with me today! At the time, I did not know about the 10,000-Hour Rule from Malcolm Gladwell's book *Outliers*. I didn't have to, because I was already hooked on doing this for the rest of my life! But that event was a turning point for me, when a mentor saw my potential to reach a higher skill level.

When I entered eighth grade, my passion for drumming was still there. However, my parents lost a business due to a fire, and moved us to another area in the state to find work. At my new school, there was no drum mentor and not a single drum set in the band room. To make the situation worse, my parents, sister, and our dog were temporarily living in a small mobile home. Yet despite this challenge, my parents surprised me with my very own drum set! They placed it in our tiny living room between the couch, stereo system, and my mom's piano. Imagine having a teenager pounding drums every day after school in your living room! In retrospect, I'm very thankful my parents were willing to make significant sacrifices (both of their finances and peace and quiet) to support my musical passion.

When I entered high school, they strategically moved back into a house with a basement. My bedroom and drums were now (you guessed it!) in the basement sanctuary. I think my parents may have received financial donations from our former next door neighbors to speed up the move!

All this to say, the importance of people investing their time, resources, skill and patience for others to succeed is an invaluable part of life. Never take it for granted, and look for opportunities to mentor others.

*Facilitate a Lesson Learned*

Conducting a "lesson learned" session can be done in a short period of time and yield great information to pay it forward for you and others.

For example, a process-reengineering initiative was rolled out globally. Implementation was accomplished at the end of the year. At the beginning of the following year, it was important for the strategy team to step back and reflect on lessons learned. What made the session impactful was the fact that they invited project team leaders who were managing new upcoming projects.

We set a target to get a minimum of five big lessons learned that would help these future project leaders. The outcome was successful! Everyone at the lessons-learned session walked away with more than anticipated.

*Paying it forward in Action - No Quality, No Business!*
*Kery's story*

My wife and I were privileged to be part of a mission trip to Kenya. One of the places we visited was the Kibera slum in Nairobi, which is the largest urban slum in Africa. We were introduced to a woman named Eunice, who chose to live there, in the midst of great poverty, as she manages a program providing job skills and encouragement to widows. Eunice and her husband named their ministry St. Martha's, after a lady named Martha (from Indiana) who took time to pay it forward by providing them start-up funds.

Upon entering their small metal-roofed shack, we were greeted by nine widows being mentored by Eunice. They were being taught new skills, such as jewelry-making and sewing, enabling them to support their families. Their products were known for their excellent quality and value. The women shared their stories with us, which included significant adversities they face on an ongoing basis. They also shared with us their hope for themselves and their children.

After hearing their stories, I asked Eunice *"How do you compete with other vendors who make jewelry and clothes? What differentiates your products from others?"* Without skipping a beat, Eunice looked at me and said a simple phrase, *"No Quality – No Business"*. She clearly understood that her mentoring must instill a high level of skill in short order for the women to produce quality products that enable them to support their families.

Eunice lives BOLD! She has determination and character. Any successful company would hire her immediately for her leadership skills and pay-it-forward mindset. She cares deeply for others and is determined to help people in difficult situations. Eunice also finished her graduate degree in business management while supporting her own family. She is fiercely focused on paying it forward. She shares best practices with others to help others overcome significant challenges.

**BOLD people who accept difficult assignments will achieve extraordinary results.**

In summary, I left changed after spending time with this exceptional person with a quiet, yet powerful demeanor. I gained significant insight about being a BOLD mentor after hearing these women's stories.

*Lessons Learned*

- Never underestimate the power of BOLD.
- Smart innovative people thrive in very difficult circumstances.
- Mentoring without application is just plain wasteful.

- Accepting challenges and adversity is a powerful trigger for growth.
- BOLD people who accept difficult assignments will achieve extraordinary results.

*Reader Reflection*

- *Who would you offer a "day in the life" event as a way of paying it forward?*
- *How do you share your lessons learned with others?*
- *Who are your mentors? What are you learning from them?*
- *Is there anyone who would name their company after you?*

## CHAPTER RE-CAP – PAYING IT FORWARD

As mentioned in the opening quote from Picasso, "The meaning of life is to find your gift. The purpose of life is to give it away."

The chapter describes four tested ideas for paying it forward

1. Host a "Day in the Life" event
2. Allow your team to *play up*
3. Facilitate a "Lessons Learned" session
4. Provide active mentoring & coaching

# CHAPTER 10
## TOOLS WORKBOOK

- Terms and Definitions
- Performance-Eating Rabbits Glossary
- Bar Napkin Exercise
- Issue/Description
- Create a Robust Strategy in Four Hours
  - Official Truth vs. Ground Truth
  - Magic Wand / Desired State
  - Rapid Gap Analysis (RGA)
  - Modified SWOT and SWOT Map
  - 21 Activity – Speed Dating for Solutions
  - Culture Pulse
  - Impact Map

| TERMS AND DEFINITIONS | |
|---|---|
| **Term** | **Definition** |
| Bar napkin | Multi-purpose tool essential for Ledge Walking Technology, or an effective moisture barrier to rest your drink on. |

| Term | Definition |
|---|---|
| BOLD | A simple acronym that provides a framework for describing the behaviors exemplar strategists exhibit while driving results that can and should be achieved in their organization. BOLD is simply:<br><br>**B** – Be authentic in your core values – regardless of your circumstances<br>**O** – Open-minded to new ideas and ways of thinking<br>**L** – Lead with courage and humility<br>**D** – Define new standards for excellence and performance in yourself and others. |
| Culture Pulse | A rapid method to assess and quantify the thoughts and feelings of a group. |
| Desired State | A state of achieving worthy performance (aka. Vision/Mission). |
| Difference Maker | The opposite of order taker. |
| Impact Map | A simple and powerful method to create a clear line of sight from competency, behaviors, results and desired state. |
| Internal Factor Evaluation (IFE) | The IFE matrix compares the internal strengths and weaknesses of the team, and provides a numeric score showing the overall health of the team and their ability to capitalize on their opportunities or protect themselves from their threats. |
| Interrogate Reality | An efficient method used to identify the official truth versus ground truth for the current state of an issue. |

| Term | Definition |
|---|---|
| External Factor Evaluation (EFE) | The EFE matrix compares the external opportunities and threats of the team and provides a numeric score that highlights what the team needs to prioritize in their strategies and goals. |
| Magic Wand | A tool used to create a pain free vision and mission that can be purchased at any dollar store. |
| Modified SWOT | A process to ensure that your strategies and goals are aligned with your current state capabilities and the pressing things in your environment. |
| Rapid Gap Analysis | An effective and efficient tool used to perform a systemic cause analysis to a given issue. |
| SME | Subject Matter Expert

Alternate definition: *Someone Management Elected* |
| Speed Dating for Solutions -21 Activity | A rapid method to minimize bias used to generate, prioritize and estimate the effort and benefit of solutions. |
| Squirrel Syndrome | The act of losing focus on the strategic task at hand when a new and seemingly real cool idea runs right in front of us. This is the human version of how dogs stop everything and anything they are doing to chase a squirrel. |
| SWOT Map | The SWOT Map enables you to demonstrate direct alignment of the strategies and goals of the team to the strengths, weaknesses, opportunities and threats that you have just analyzed. |

## PERFORMANCE-EATING RABBITS GLOSSARY

| Performance-Eating Rabbit | Definition |
|---|---|
| Political Rabbit | Tends to be out in front of other PERs. Promotes their flavor of the month and exerts power in action and the ability to influence outcomes. |
| Hasty Hopper | Focused on doing the expedient thing over the right thing. They achieve efficiency and speed in whatever they do. They reward teams who achieve short wins and reward the workforce with more work; creating low retention, fear or distrust. |
| One-Hit-Wonder Wabbit | Frequently supports one solution (their solution) for any initiative. They fail to see the larger system or consider blended solutions to correct an issue. |
| Bias Bunny | Tame on the outside but may have a passive/aggressive attitude for new innovative solutions. They go to great lengths to discredit the ideas of others. |
| Complacent Bunny | They will participate in teams but will not significantly contribute. They shy away from making waves or having challenging conversations. |

| Performance-Eating Rabbit | Definition |
|---|---|
| Culture Rabbit | Largest of the PER family. Has an overwhelming ability to prevent the right culture from taking hold. They are skilled and experienced at maintaining status quo and will challenge the positive elements of your strategy. |
| Ledge Walking Rabbit | They have the desire to see the organization flourish but may not have the tools to make the right changes necessary for success. They easily succumb to the "Squirrel Syndrome" and will jump over to a *more shiny* initiative when the going get's tough. |

## Bar Napkin Exercise

*Introduction and Purpose:*

The purpose of this tool is to create an open reflection for leaders to think about the work they are doing, the solutions they are implementing, and the perception of the solution as it relates to business impact.

*Steps to complete the Bar Napkin Exercise*
(estimated total time=20 minutes)

| Step | Action |
|------|--------|
| 1 | Introduce the activity by providing each participant a bar napkin. |
| 2 | Draw lines on your napkin into four sections and label:<br><br>• Initiatives<br>• Solutions<br>• Tax, Staff Benefit, Business Driver<br>• Key Behaviors |
| 3 | Ask participants to identify and record the top three to five initiatives they are currently working on in the first section of the napkin. |
| 4 | Ask participants to identify and record the solution for each initiative in the second section:<br><br>• I = Instructional (training solution)<br>• NI= Non-instructional solution (improved process, increased pay)<br>• BL= Blended solution (combination of instructional and non-instructional |
| 5 | Ask participants to identify how their solution will be perceived by the target audience for each initiative:<br><br>• Tax= Perceived as another activity to do; costing time or money<br>• Staff benefit = perceived as a benefit to the employee<br>• Business Driver = Perceived as important to improve our business outcomes |
| 6 | Ask participants to share the initiatives that are perceived as business drivers? |
| 7 | Allow participants to reflect on what they wrote down. Ask them what actions they would personally take after completing their bar napkin? |

## BAR NAPKIN EXERCISE - EXAMPLE

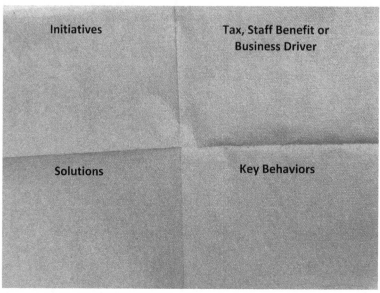

© Performance Journey Partners, LLC

## BAR NAPKIN EXERCISE – COMPLETED EXAMPLE

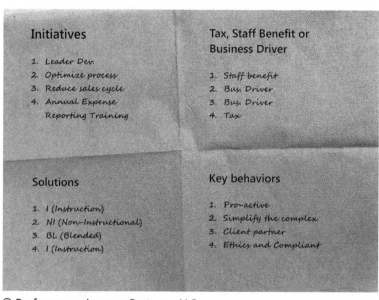

© Performance Journey Partners, LLC

## Issue/Description

### Issue Description Tool

As previously mentioned, the Issue Description Tool is our adaptation of the tool from Susan Scott's book "*Fierce Conversations*." Susan does a great job of providing a simple tool to define the issue you are working on, the importance of the issue, and then (clearly and humbly) request the assistance you are seeking. The only subtle, yet impactful, change we've made to her process is to add an additional emphasis on the urgency of the issue we are working on. Too many times, we blur the lines of significance and urgency. The sheer fact that we need something now does not make it significant. The following is the template we use.

| Criteria | Issue Definition |
|---|---|
| THE ISSUE IS: | |
| IT IS SIGNIFICANT BECAUSE: | |
| THE URGENCY OF THIS ISSUE IS: | |
| MY IDEAL OUTCOME IS: | |
| RELEVANT BACKGROUND INFORMATION: | |
| WHAT I HAVE DONE UP TO THIS POINT: | |
| THE HELP I WANT FROM YOU IS: | |

## CREATE A ROBUST STRATEGY IN FOUR HOURS

| Tool | Outcome | ~Time (Mins) |
|------|---------|--------------|
| **Official Truth vs. Ground Truth** | Interrogate Reality | 15 |
| **Magic Wand/Desired State** | Pain free vision statement | 20 |
| **Rapid Gap Analysis (RGA)** | Categorize Causal Factors | 45 |
| **Modified SWOT** | Guide Leader Actions | 60 |
| **21 Activity – Speed Dating for Solutions** | Target Solutions | 30 |
| **Culture Pulse** | Assess Change Readiness | 10 |
| ***Impact Map** | Build Behavioral Bridge | 40 |
| **Executive Summary** | Summarize Strategy | 20 |

*Note: Completing an Impact Map is an optional activity when completing the Four-Hour Strategy.

## OFFICIAL TRUTH VS. GROUND TRUTH

*Introduction & Purpose:*

Interrogating reality is a simple and effective tool used to understand the underlying thoughts and feelings of individuals, teams or work groups. It allows one to capture and differentiate official truth from the ground truth. Without assessing the ground truth, you will waste precious time and regurgitate the next "flavor of the month." You also may lose your credibility with the people who want to see meaningful change happen.

Completing this exercise with groups allows participants to say what the real problem is in a respectful way. When we run this activity, we encourage every work group to "applaud wildly" after each group shares their feedback. This allows recognition that the transparency which exists can be an excellent precursor to trust. We recommend posting their results on the wall during the session. This creates a fence in the room to prevent *Performance-Eating Rabbits* from entering the sacred space.

*Steps to complete Interrogate Reality (Official Vs. Ground Truth)* (estimated time=15 minutes)

| Step | Action |
|------|--------|
| 1 | Provide participants several examples that describe official truth vs. ground truth. Have some fun with this and start with a personal example. (i.e. Tim's Official Truth: In my house I'm in charge 100% of the time. Ground Truth: My wife is in charge 95% of the time and my daughter the remaining 5%) |
| 2 | Provide each working group a flip chart and markers. Appoint a scribe for each group to capture the information. |
| 3 | Provide the groups 7-10 minutes to discuss and summarize their official and ground truth statements. (example provided). |
| 4 | Ask a representative from each work group to share their results. Make sure to have the overall team applaud wildly after each debrief to keep a safe and open environment. |
| 5 | Collect each group's information and load into your summary deck. |

## OFFICIAL VS. GROUND TRUTH - COMPLETED EXAMPLE

| Official Truth | Ground Truth |
|---|---|
| We hire, onboard, and set clear expectations | We do not provide enough experiential learning to keep them engaged |
| Decisions on the organizational strategy are made from top down | Middle managers are not owning the solution; not empowering themselves |
| There are many learning opportunities | We are too busy with day-to-day; not effective use of time |
| Work/life balance | Work actually out-balances life |
| We develop employees | There are limited development opportunities |
| Sustainability | Sustainability is not strong |
| We have career paths | Limited career path |
| Strong leaders | No evidence of leaders |
| Strong performance management | Our feedback is not effective |

## MAGIC WAND / DESIRED STATE

### Introduction & Purpose:

Creating the desired state is essential to get everyone's thoughts and ideas locked into a statement that describes their ideal vision. Starting with the end in mind is critical.

Using the magic wand helps clients step out of the environmental focus and into the future state. It can be completed with small, medium and large audiences in twenty minutes. Creating the desired state is an activity that works best with two facilitators; one facilitating the activity and the second person decoding the information. If you are creating an organizational strategy, we recommend doing this activity after interrogating reality.

Lastly, it tends to be a very fun activity – so make sure you stock up on magic wands! Using this approach will minimize the effect of *Performance-Eating Rabbits* – namely the *Culture, One-Hit-Wonder Wabbit* and *Political Rabbit*. The *Hasty Hopper* will be your friend since the process is efficient.

*Steps to complete a Pain-free Vison Statement*
(estimated time 20 mins)

| Step | Action |
|------|--------|
| 1 | Invite a group of involved stakeholders and participants. <br><br> Provide Post-It Notes to each table. Tell them they will record individual responses on a Post-It. |
| 2 | Introduce the purpose of creating their desired state. <br><br> Select a volunteer who is most interested in waving a magic wand. |
| 3 | Ask the individual with the magic wand to wave it over the audience in the room. |
| 4 | Tell participants, since the magic wand has now been waved, their desired state has occurred. Have them imagine the vision for their team has now become reality. <br><br> (ask participants the following suggested questions). <br><br> • What does this desired state look like? <br> • What would people be saying about it? <br> • What leading indicators would be in place? <br> • What are the new results realized? <br> • What are our customers saying about us? <br> • What is our staff saying about us? <br> • What are our competitors saying about us? <br> • How do I feel about being a part of this team or organization? <br> • How do we measure our new-found success? |

| Step | Action |
|------|--------|
| 6 | One facilitator collects the Post It Notes from participants while the other facilitator categorizes the feedback and begins blended coding (open & axial) and creating the desired state on a flip chart. |
| 7 | Conduct the reveal by sharing their desired state with the participants at the end of the exercise. |

## DESIRED STATE BLENDING CODING EXAMPLE

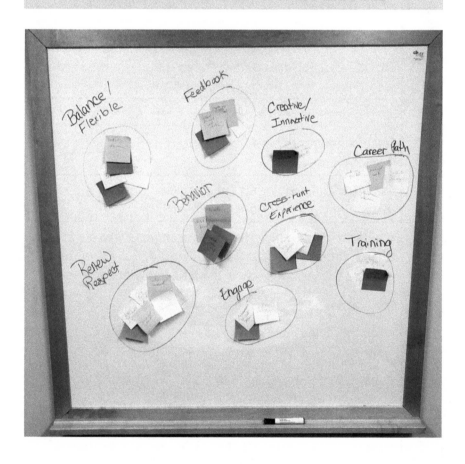

## DESIRED STATE - COMPLETED EXAMPLE

*Our mid-level managers will cultivate an innovative and balanced workplace where they provide frequent feedback and coaching with project-based learning and team engagement.*

*They will demonstrate respect for the value each millennial brings to the organization by proactively learning about new technologies, and engaging in reverse mentoring by co-creating a career map.*

## RAPID GAP ANALYSIS (RGA)

### Introduction & Purpose:

Facilitating an RGA session is relatively easy. Using a set of targeted powerful questions, responses will uncover specific factors causing the problem, or preventing your current solutions from working. The RGA also illuminates factors that can allow success of your initiative. In addition, you also receive the gift of a qualitative rating for each of the six cell categories.

The materials you will need are a flip chart and colored markers. We typically use red, orange (in place of yellow for visibility) and green markers for each table. We recommend having table groups of 4-6 participants to enhance dialog and discussion.

*Steps to complete the Rapid Gap Analysis*
(estimated total time= 45 minutes)

| Step | Action |
|------|--------|
| 1 | Identify and invite individuals close to the issue to attend the one hour RGA meeting. |
| 2 | Provide a brief introduction of the RGA purpose. Appoint a table leader and scribe for each table. Provide each participant the RGA Job Aid. |

| Step | Action |
|------|--------|
| 3 | Allow each table group 30 minutes to complete the exercise. Ask each table leader to initiate discussion with their table group using the list of questions. The scribe at each table will capture the responses onto a flip chart. |
| 4 | The table leader asks them to color code each six-cell box to indicate the severity of the gap (Major=Red, Moderate=Yellow/Orange and Minor=Green):<br><br>• Red indicates major gaps that will impede the desired outcome.<br>• Yellow/Orange indicates moderate gaps that could impede the desired outcome.<br>• Green indicates few or no gaps with little to no impact to the desired outcome. |
| 6 | After each table leader shares their feedback, encourage the entire room to "applaud wildly" for their table. We also like to verbally recognize the table leader and scribe for their heroic work. |
| 7 | At this point, we have participants take a short break. We take their flip charts and transfer their data into a six-cell template. |

## TEMPLATE FOR RGA

| Information | Instrumentation | Motivation | |
|-------------|-----------------|------------|---|
| DATA | INSTRUMENTS | INCENTIVES | |
| | | | Rooted in the Environment/ Organization |
| KNOWLEDGE | CAPACITY | MOTIVES | |
| | | | Rooted in the Individual Worker |

## RGA Job Aid – Environmental Factors

| Environmental Factors | | |
|---|---|---|
| **Data** | **Instruments** | **Incentives** |
| What are expectations of the workforce (target audience)? | What word or phrase would you use to indicate the current work environment? | What are the rewards for achieving exceptional performance? |
| Are the workforce expectations clear and measurable? | Are departments adequately staffed to perform the work? | What are the career advancement opportunities for an exemplar performer? |
| Where do individuals go to find answers for performing their work? Does the support help or hinder their success? | What tools or instruments help or hinder completion of the work?<br><br>Are the procedures and processes for completing the work efficient and effective? | What is the perception of the incentive system? Does the workforce know the incentives exist? |
| What metrics and/or feedback is used to monitor worker performance? Are your current metrics leading or lagging indicators? | What actions establish the perfect environment for your workforce? | What consequences are in place for poor performance? Are they used? Does the workforce know the consequences for poor performance exist? |
| What documents (or information) support their performance? | Can the worker/team realistically complete the required tasks (work) in the time allotted? | How is success of the incentive system measured? |

©Performance Journey Partners, LLC

## RGA JOB AID – INDIVIDUAL FACTORS

| Individual Worker Factors | | |
|---|---|---|
| **Knowledge** | **Capacity** | **Motives** |
| How is the target audience trained to perform their role? Is it effective and/or efficient?<br><br>How is the target audience trained to report and correct potential mistakes in their work?<br><br>What knowledge and skills are critical for the performer to deliver high quality service or results?<br><br>What are the key behaviors that support the performance you desire?<br><br>Does your workforce demonstrate those behaviors? | What standard selection criteria is used to hire a team member in this role?<br><br>How do typical workers feel at the end of their shift/ work experience?<br><br>What specific experiences and attributes do you look for in selecting a job candidate?<br><br>How does the expected work align to the department's mission?<br><br>What are the current employee retention metrics for this role? | How would you rate the current motivation of the team members?<br><br>How do team members motivate each other to "be on their game"?<br><br>How do they stay motivated to provide the exceptional service you provide?<br><br>What derailers exist that could impair team motivation?<br><br>What word describes worker attitude? |

©Performance Journey Partners, LLC

## RGA Summary - Completed Example

| Major Gaps |
| Moderate Gaps |
| Few or None |

| Information | Instrumentation | Motivation |
|---|---|---|
| **DATA** | **INSTRUMENTS/ RESOURCES** | **INCENTIVES** |
| • Inconsistent systems of records<br>• Development and expectations are not aligned<br>• Individual performance not connected to org performance<br>• Data not being used<br>• Focus is more on lagging measures<br>• Meetings are not efficient | • Current processes don't align to bigger picture<br>• Reactive vs proactive<br>• Traditional environment is 'old school'<br>• We don't invest in the right tools to meet the work capacity | • Bonus (annual)<br>• Merit increase<br>• Peer to peer recognition programs<br>• Salary not matching work load<br>• Work/life flexibility jeopardized |
| **KNOWLEDGE** | **CAPACITY** | **MOTIVES** |
| • Some Online / e-learning; not engaging<br>• Some mentoring<br>• No measurement of effectiveness | • Slow to make hiring decisions<br>• Recruiting to core competencies<br>• High retention of mid-managers | • There are international opportunities for high performers<br>• High engagement<br>• Not clear how opportunities are awarded |

## Modified SWOT

*Introduction & Purpose:*

The Modified SWOT analysis process will ensure that your strategies and goals are aligned with your current state capabilities and the pressing things in your environment.

*Steps to complete a Modified SWOT*
(estimated total time=1 hour)

| Step | Action |
|------|--------|
| 1 | Ask the team to share what they feel are the strengths, weaknesses, opportunities and threats for their team in the context of the vision they are pursuing. |
| 2 | Complete the IFE matrix and summary. |
| 3 | Complete the EFE matrix and summary. |
| 4 | Complete the SWOT map. |
| 5 | Share the modified SWOT summary with the team. |
| 6 | Include the modified SWOT summary with the overall strategy deck. |

## EXTERNAL FACTORS EVALUATION (EFE) - COMPLETED EXAMPLE

| Critical Success Factors | Weight | Rating | Weighted Score |
|---|---|---|---|
| Opportunities | | | |
| Learning from millennial | 0.13 | 1.7 | 0.22 |
| Form mutually beneficial partnership to drive innovation | 0.17 | 1.8 | 0.31 |
| Increase the ability to attract millennials | 0.20 | 1.8 | 0.36 |
| Educate midlevel managers to share their knowledge and experience | 0.13 | 1.8 | 0.23 |
| Redefine relevant retention targets for millennials | 0.08 | 1.5 | 0.12 |
| Threats | | | |
| High Turnover (cost) | 0.17 | 1.7 | 0.29 |
| Brand Damage | 0 | 1.7 | 0.00 |
| Stalling new innovation | 0.12 | 1.3 | 0.16 |
| Threat to sustain industries | 0 | 2.7 | 0.00 |
| TOTAL | 1 | | 1.69 |

©Performance Journey Partners, LLC

The External Factor Evaluation (EFE) indicates that strategies and action plans need to focus on mitigating the threats identified prior to focusing on the identified opportunities. Mitigating the cost and stalling of innovation resulting from millennial turnover require immediate solutions.

## INTERNAL FACTORS EVALUATION (IFE) - COMPLETED EXAMPLE

| Critical Success Factors | Weight | Rating | Weighted Score |
|---|---|---|---|
| **Strengths** | | | |
| Knowledge of Patients | 0.01 | 2 | 0.03 |
| Experience | 0.10 | 3.3 | 0.33 |
| Commitment | 0.09 | 3.4 | 0.30 |
| Passion for work | 0.11 | 3 | 0.33 |
| Knowledge of manufacturing process | 0.09 | 3 | 0.28 |
| Closer to ground truth | 0.03 | 2.5 | 0.07 |
| **Weakness** | | | |
| Pulse on our customers | 0.04 | 1.5 | 0.06 |
| Prioritization (lack of) | 0.11 | 1.3 | 0.15 |
| Courage to say no – focus on priorities | 0.07 | 1.6 | 0.11 |
| Decisive decision making | 0.07 | 1.7 | 0.13 |
| Making a decision stick & sustain | 0.07 | 1.6 | 0.12 |
| Bureaucracy | 0.11 | 1.2 | 0.13 |
| Sole source knowledge centrality | 0.02 | 1.7 | 0.04 |
| Contingent labor strategy | 0.08 | 1.5 | 0.12 |
| **TOTAL** | **1** | | **2.2** |

©Performance Journey Partners, LLC

The Internal Factor Evaluation (IFE) indicates that our community is operating from a solid place of strength. While the lack of flexibility, willingness to explore new technology and general fear are key concerns we share about our mid-level managers, their high level of commitment and overall knowledge provide a solid platform to strategically leverage strengths.

## SWOT MAP - COMPLETED EXAMPLE

| | Strengths | Weakness |
|---|---|---|
| | 7. Technical Knowledge<br>8. Organizational Knowledge<br>9. Structured Process<br>10. Aware of Blind Spot<br>11. Committed to Organization<br>12. Business Acumen | 7. Little Flexibility<br>8. Fear (Displacement, change, new workplace)<br>9. Technology Deficiencies<br>10. Lack of Trust<br>11. Exasperation<br>12. Don't acknowledge/recognize value millennials |
| **Opportunities** | **S-O Strategies** | **W-O Strategies** |
| 6. Learning from millennial<br>7. Form mutually beneficial partnerships<br>8. Increase the ability to attract millennials<br>9. Educate midlevel managers to share knowledge and experience<br>10. Redefine relevant retention targets for millennials | 3. Set up partnerships to learn from one another; across generations (S1, S2, S3, S5, O2, O4)<br>4. Social events with mid-managers and Millennials (S3, S5, O1, O2) | 3. Mini town-halls within departments. Getting more feedback from the analyst level (W2, W4, W5, W6, O1, O4)<br>4. Managers will have frequent focus group session with direct reports to get feedback & suggestions (W2, W4, W5, W6, O1, O4) |
| **Threats** | **S-T Strategies** | **W-T Strategies** |
| 5. High turnover (cost)<br>6. Brand Damage<br>7. Stalling new innovation<br>8. Threat to sustain industries | 2. Create a leadership development program for Millennials with action learning projects sponsored by Mid-Managers (S1, S2, S5, S6, T1) | 2. Training/education for managers (W1, W2, W3, T1, T3) |

## 21 ACTIVITY (SPEED DATING FOR SOLUTIONS)

*Introduction & Purpose:*

This activity will generate, analyze, and prioritize ideas on a given topic using collaborative inquiry. The materials you will need are the 21 Activity handout that includes the instructions, a train whistle or your favorite noise maker.

*Steps to complete the 21 Activity (Speed Dating for Solutions)* (estimated total time=30 minutes)

| Step | Action |
|------|--------|
| 1 | First, invite a group of participants who are seeking solutions to an issue. To build excitement, we suggest doing this activity not in a conference room, but in a location of their choice. *Their budget will determine their options. |
| 2 | After describing the purpose of the tool, provide the 21 Activity handout and review instructions for the exercise. |
| 3 | Ask each participant to write down their idea/solution that will fix the issue or eliminate the cause for a given problem in the box provided in the handout. |
| 4 | After everyone has recorded their idea, ask them to exchange their idea with someone else in the room. This step is critical.<br><br>Tell participants the gift you have received is now your solution for the rest of the exercise. |
| 6 | Ask everyone to form groups of three and give instructions on how to dialog and score each idea. To make it easy, we show by example how a round is played.<br><br>In groups of three, each person shares their idea verbally in a speedy manner. Then discuss each of the solutions and score each idea using a maximum of 3 points for the best idea, 2 points for the second best and 1 point for the remaining idea. Each person then records their score in Round 1 of your handout. Don't worry if there is a group of 4; the fourth best idea also gets 1 point.<br><br>After scoring the ideas, ask them to estimate the amount of effort and benefit (using Low, Moderate or High) and again record the results for your idea under the appropriate Effort/Benefit column for the specific round. |

| Step | Action |
|------|--------|
| 7 | Once everyone has finished the first round, pull out your trusty train whistle and blow loudly. Tell participants to connect with two new people and begin the round two. The pace of the exercise gets faster each round as networking their idea with others gains momentum. Continue each round in the same fashion until the group has completed seven rounds. You may choose to play fewer rounds based on the number of participants. Collect all the handouts and transfer the data to the 21 Activity summary report. |

## 21 ACTIVITY – SPEED DATING FOR SOLUTIONS

*This activity will generate, analyze, and prioritize ideas on a given topic using collaborative inquiry.*

### Step 1: Capture your idea.

Take a minute to generate a solution for achieving our desired state...

| Idea/Solution: |
|---|
| |
| |
| |

### Step 2: Exchange idea w/someone else.

After exchanging your idea, take a moment to ensure you understand the solution you now hold. Note: You will retain this new solution throughout each scoring activity during step 3.

## Step 3: Participate in scoring activity.

Share and discuss the idea you have with two fellow colleagues. Rate/score each idea for this round using a maximum of **3 points for the best idea, 2 points for the second-best idea and 1 point for remaining idea(s)** and record the score of this idea in the box below. If there is a group of 4; the fourth best idea also gets 1 point.

Rate and record the level of effort and benefit for each idea (**H**=High, **M**=Moderate, **L**=Low) in the box below.

After the scoring for the round is complete, seek out two new people and repeat the process.

|  | Idea Score (3/2/1) | Effort (H/M/L) | Benefit (H/M/L) |
|---|---|---|---|
| Round 1 |  |  |  |
| Round 2 |  |  |  |
| Round 3 |  |  |  |
| Round 4 |  |  |  |
| Round 5 |  |  |  |
| Round 6 |  |  |  |
| Round 7 |  |  |  |
|  | Total: | Avg. | Avg. |

## 21 ACTIVITY SUMMARY REPORT

| # | Idea/Solution | Score | Effort/Benefit<br>L=Low M=Mod H=High |
|---|---|---|---|
| (1) | Create a leadership development program for millennials with action learning projects sponsored by mid-managers | 19 | H/H |
| (2) | Set up partnerships to learn from one another (across the generations). | 17 | M/H |
| (3) | Mini town-halls within departments. Getting more feedback from the analyst level. | 16 | L/M |
| (4) | Managers will have frequent focus group session with direct reports to get feedback & suggestions | 10 | L/M |
| (5) | Training for managers (education) | 8 | H/H |
| (6) | Social events with mid-managers and millennials | 7 | L/L |

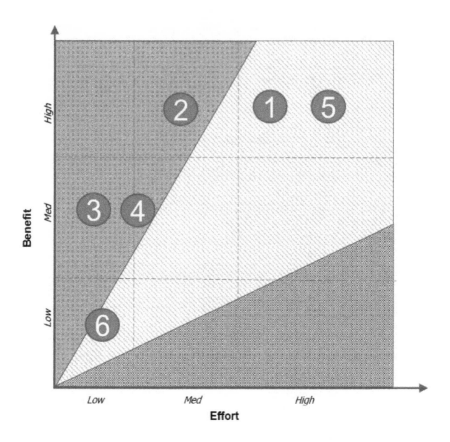

## CULTURE PULSE

### Introduction & Purpose:

This tool is beneficial at the start of an important initiative to get a pulse on thoughts and feelings of key stakeholders, and/or a new team that is forming.

*Steps to complete the Culture Pulse*
(estimated total time=10 minutes)

| Step | Action |
|------|--------|
| 1 | Introduce the topic on thoughts and feelings with your target audience. |
| 2 | Hand out the paper copy or electronic survey, with the instruction to circle or check all the thoughts and feelings from the list. |
| 3 | After participants have completed the pulse check, pull the data and complete a Pareto chart as shown in the Culture Pulse example. |
| 4 | Based on the feedback received, provide the team or stakeholders the chart with your summary of the results. |

Note: You may choose to complete the same activity at a later point in time to see what changes may have occurred.

## PULSE SURVEY

Please circle the words or phrases that best describe your thoughts and feelings.

| | | | |
|---|---|---|---|
| Afraid | Doubtful | Interested | Scared |
| Against It | Energized | Irate | Settled |
| Angry | Excited | Isolated | Shy |
| Anxious | Excluded | Nervous | Skeptical |
| Capable | Friendly | Proactive | Supportive |
| Challenged | Happy | Ready | Uncertain |
| Comfortable | Helpful | Relieved | Uninterested |
| Confident | Hopeful | Respected | Unprepared |
| Confused | Included | Reactive | Upset |
| Disrespected | Informed | Sad | Valued |

© Performance Journey Partners, LLC

## CULTURE PULSE EXAMPLE

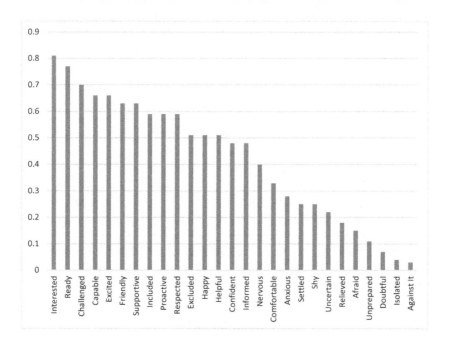

*The culture pulse highlights the interest, readiness, confidence and excitement of the team. It also indicated the team's positive sense of being included and respected.*

## IMPACT MAP

### Introduction & Purpose:

Impact Maps help take the guesswork out of culture work by isolating the few critical behaviors that will deliver results and support the goals for your initiative.

The materials you will need:

Computer with an electronic Impact Map is optional. Flip chart and markers will do just as well.

Note: We recommend using a four column Impact Map template. We suggest co-facilitating this activity; one person facilitates the discussion and another person records the information into the Impact Map template.

*Steps to complete*
(estimated total time=1 hour)

| Step | Action |
|------|--------|
| 1 | When scheduling the Impact Map session, select leaders and team members who clearly understand the goal of the initiative. Identify and add the name of the target audience at the top of the page of your Impact Map template. |
| 2 | Enter the goal statement into the far-right column of the template. If the goal is still undefined, have the discussion first to clarify the goal (or desired state) with participants. This is key, as you want to start with the end in mind. |
| 3 | Ask participants to identify key results that would provide evidence the goal has been achieved (or not). Spend the time and effort necessary to uncover predictive indicators. Results can be either individual or team results. Record the results in the appropriate column of the Impact Map template. |
| 4 | Ask participants to identify key behaviors they believe would contribute to the results. Key behaviors are those that will support multiple results. Record the results in the appropriate column of the Impact Map template. |
| 5 | After you have the list of behaviors recorded, brainstorm a list of knowledge or skills that enable and support the key behaviors for the target audience. Record the results in the appropriate column of the Impact Map template. |

| Step | Action |
|------|--------|
| 6 | Once the Impact Map is drafted, we validate the Impact Map using story-telling. We ask each participant to share a story that describes what knowledge and skills are essential to support key behaviors. Then describe which behaviors have the most impact on results. Lastly, what results are essential to indicate we have attained the goal. |
| 7 | Capture your final results for each column after completing validation. |

Note: Completing an Impact Map is an optional activity when completing the Four-Hour Strategy.

### IMPACT MAP - COMPLETED EXAMPLE

| Knowledge and Skills | Key Behaviors | Key Results | Desired State |
|---|---|---|---|
| • Blended listening skills<br>• Coaching / Reverse-Mentoring<br>• Risk management<br>• Learn technology (i.e. social media)<br>• Increase knowledge of work policies<br>• Constructive feedback skills | O Proactive Feedback and communication<br>O Flexibility (where, when and how)<br>O Encourage creativity and innovation<br>O Challenge millennials with stretch assignments<br>O Seek to actively learn from millennials | ✓ Reduced millennial turnover<br>✓ Increased millennial referrals<br>✓ Increased millennial retention<br>✓ Increased and improved development opportunities and outcomes<br>✓ Increased 'Glass Door' recommendations | Our mid-level managers will cultivate an innovative and balanced workplace, where they provide frequent feedback and coaching, project-based learning to drive engagement.<br><br>They will demonstrate respect for the value each millennial brings to the organization by proactively learning about new technologies and engaging in reverse mentoring |

# References:

Implementation – The Glue of Organizational Change; Roger M. Addison and Clayton R. Lloyd

Harvard Business Review, The Making of an Expert by K. Anders Ericsson, Michael J. Prietula, and Edward T. Cokely

Leading Strategic Execution; Advantage Performance Group

Fierce Conversations; Susan Scott; Berkley Books 2002

Human Capital Analytics, Harness the Potential of Your Organization's Greatest Asset; Gene Pease, Boyce Byerly, Jac Fitz-enz; Published by John Wiley and Sons 2013

Telling Training's Story – Evaluation Made Simple, Credible, and Effective; Robert O. Brinkerhoff; Berrett-Koehler Publishers Inc. 2006

The Performance Consultant's Fieldbook; Judith Hale; Pfeiffer, Second Edition 2007

Fundamentals of Performance Technology; Darlene M. Van Tiem, James L. Mosely, Joan Conway Dessinger; International Society of Performance Improvement Washington D.C. 2000

Performance Improvement Interventions; Darlene M. Van Tiem, James L. Mosely, Joan Conway Dessinger; International Society of Performance Improvement Washington D.C. 2000

Outliers - The Story of Success; Malcolm Gladwell; Little, Brown and Company;

Give and Take; A Revolutionary Approach To Success; Adam Grant;

Viking Published by the Penguin Group Penguin Group(USA) Inc., 375 Hudson Street, New York, New York 10014, USA

DRiVE - The Surprising Truth About What Motivates Us; Daniel H. Pink; RIVERHEAD BOOKS Published by the Penguin Group 2009

Six Conversations – A Simple Guide for Managerial Success; Steve King; iUniverse 2015

Crucial Conversations – Tools for Talking When Stakes are High Second Edition; Patterson, Grenny, McMillan, Switzler; McGraw Hill 2012

Organizational Consulting – How to Be an Effective Internal Change Agent; Alan Weiss, PhD.; John Wiley and Sons Inc.2003

Essentials of Organizational Behavior; Eighth Edition; Stephen P. Robbins; Pearson Prentice Hall 2005

Fundamentals of Performance Technology; Darlene M. Van Tiem, James L. Mosely, Joan Conway Dessinger; International Society for Performance Improvement 2000

Performance Improvement Interventions; Darlene M. Van Tiem, James L. Mosely, Joan Conway Dessinger; International Society for Performance Improvement 2001

The Five Dysfunctions of a Team; Patrick Lencioni; Josey Bass 2002

The Power of Story; Jim Loehr; Free Press 2007

Barking Up the Wrong Tree; Eric Barker; Harper Collins Publishers; 2017